DOUBLE TAKE
Two sides One story

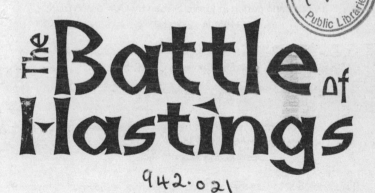

The Battle of Hastings

CHRIS PRIESTLEY

For Robbie

This story is based, as much as possible, on primary source material - the words and
pictures of the people that witnessed the events described. Whilst it is not possible to
know the exact thoughts, feelings and motives of all the people involved, the book aims
to give an insight into the experience of the events, based on the available evidence.

Scholastic Children's Books
Commonwealth House, 1–19 New Oxford Street,
London, WC1A 1NU, UK
A division of Scholastic Ltd
London ~ New York ~ Toronto ~ Sydney ~ Auckland
Mexico City ~ New Delhi ~ Hong Kong

Published in the UK by Scholastic Ltd, 2003

ISBN 0 439 98241 3

Printed and bound in Great Britain by Cox & Wyman,
Reading, Berkshire

Cover image: Replica of the Bayeux Tapestry Copyright Reading
Museum Service (Reading Borough Council). All rights reserved.

2 4 6 8 10 9 7 5 3 1

Contents

Prologue

SOMETIME AROUND 1090, a beautiful new work of art was created. On to a 70-metre-long piece of linen, a sort of early strip cartoon was skilfully sewn in coloured threads. The borders show all kinds of fabulous creatures and hunting scenes, but the main images are full of axe-wielding warriors, flying arrows, painted shields and galloping war-horses.

The Bayeux Tapestry tells the story of two of the greatest warriors of the age – Harold Godwinson, Earl of Wessex, and William, Duke of Normandy – and their struggle for possession of the English throne. It is a struggle that ends in one of the most famous battles of all time: the Battle of Hastings.

In 1066, both men became King of England but only one *kept* the crown. Neither man was of royal blood but both claimed they were the rightful king. Who did people believe at the time and who – if anyone – was telling the truth?

There are always at least two sides to every story and the story of Harold and William, and of the Battle of Hastings, is no exception.

Harold
King of England
January 1066

IN LONDON, ON 4 JANUARY, the English king – Edward the Confessor – lay close to death in a fitful, feverish sleep, watched by his wife, Queen Edith, her brother, Harold Godwinson, a Norman courtier called Robert fitzWymark and Stigand, Archbishop of Canterbury.

They, along with all the most important people in England, had gathered at Westminster for the King's Christmas Court. The royal court was not in one fixed place at this time; it moved around the country with the King. However, Edward, with his palace at Westminster, was beginning to make London seem like the capital city it was to become. The city streets were filled with visitors, eager to be present at the consecration of Edward's beautiful new church at Westminster Abbey.

But the frail old King had fallen ill over Christmas and was forced to take to his bed. He had been in a fever for days, but on this day he seemed to be particularly agitated and those who were watching decided it might be better to wake him.

King Edward opened his eyes and told his listeners about a dream he had just had in which he had met two monks he had known in Normandy, monks who had died years before. The ghostly monks told him, among other things, that God had cursed England because of the wickedness of its earls and churchmen. Stigand, England's leading churchman, leaned over to Earl Harold and whispered that the King was clearly gibbering. Even so, the King's vision of an England abandoned by God, with devils coming through the land *with fire and sword and the havoc of war,"* must have been a little disturbing.

Edward then calmed himself and asked God to repay Queen Edith's devotion to him. He held out his hand to the Queen's brother, Harold Godwinson, and said:

> I commend this woman and all the kingdom to your protection.
> Remember that she is your lady and sister and serve her
> faithfully and honour her as such for all the days of her life. Do
> not take away from her any honour that I have granted her.

Knowing how Harold, along with most Englishmen, resented his Norman and French courtiers, the dying King also asked Harold to protect all foreigners living in England. Most important of all, the childless Edward put England under Harold's protection.

Archbishop Stigand gave Edward the last rites and he

died on 5 January – the eve of Twelfth Night. The day after, his body was carried in a procession, wearing a crown and holding a sceptre, and buried in Edward's new church. He was to become a saint and his tomb a shrine.

Harold's succession was confirmed by the *witangemot* – "the meeting of wise men" – which was a kind of committee made up of the most important people in the country. England was a long way from having an elected government as we have today, but the *witangemot* was more than most countries had at this time.

Each village in England had a village meeting or "moot" to discuss village matters and anything they could not deal with could be taken up through other, higher-level, meetings until it might just end up being discussed by the *witangemot*, which then advised the king. It was not much, but with the *witangemot* the king might catch a glimpse of what the man in the street – or at least the muddy track – was thinking. Not that he was obliged to take any notice, of course.

The *witangemot* did not choose the king, but they did have a chance to have their say before the choice was announced. It was a way of avoiding a crippling civil war. Better to find out first if the most powerful men in the country were going to object to the choice of monarch than to wait until the blood started to flow.

There were those who favoured the last surviving member of the Wessex royal line – Edgar the Aetheling he was called, meaning Edgar the Heir – he was the great-grandson of Ethelred the Unready. But, although the vote was not unanimous, the support for Harold was overwhelming. Edgar was in his early teens and the country needed strong leadership. Harold was the man for the job. The *witangemot* knew him. They knew they could count on him in a fight.

And so, on 6 January 1066 Harold Godwinson entered Westminster Abbey for his coronation, and took the oaths of kingship, promising to rule with peace, justice and mercy, and to defend the people and the church. Earl Harold was now King Harold II of England.

Edward's funeral had taken place that very morning and Harold's enemies believed that this coronation was performed with unseemly haste, but England could not be left leaderless. The country needed a king and Edward had chosen Harold as his successor, with a foreign witness – Robert fitzWymark – in the room. The English had agreed and Harold was now rightfully King of England. It all seemed fairly straightforward. Unfortunately, it was not quite so simple...

Harold was not royalty – he was only the King's brother-in-law. Edward had died without a son and heir. In 1066 a successor did not *have* to be the son of the King of England to become king, but it certainly helped. Harold's father was Earl Godwin; Harold had inherited the earldom of Wessex from him when he died.

Wessex, along with earldoms such as Mercia and

Northumbria, *had* once been a kingdom in its own right. These kingdoms had been formed by the Anglo-Saxon tribes who invaded the old province of Britannia after the fall of the Roman Empire – Wessex being the kingdom of the West Saxons. But over the centuries a new nation was forged out of these separate kingdoms – England – and a new people – the English. Earls like Godwin governed the old kingdoms in the king's name; they were given their title by the king and could have it taken away again if they were disloyal. However, Godwin was not given the earldom of Wessex by an *English* king at all, but a *Danish* one: King Cnut.

For centuries England had been at the mercy of barbarian raiders from Scandinavia that ravaged and ransacked the coastlines of Europe. Their victims gave them the name "Vikings", meaning "sea-robbers". At first these Vikings restricted themselves to smash-and-grab raids on monasteries, butchering unarmed monks and stealing the unguarded treasures they held, but eventually they saw England as a good place to settle down. In 1013 the Danes invaded in force, occupying most of East Anglia and north-east England.

Alfred the Great, the King of Wessex in the ninth century, led the resistance and the invaders were forced to stop their move west. The area they had occupied became known as the Danelaw, but eventually they were kicked out of that, too, by Alfred's descendants. England prospered again. But that only encouraged the robbers to return.

This time England did not have Alfred the Great, it had Ethelred the Unready, a weak and dithering king who tried to buy off the Danish raiders. They took the money, of course; money that Ethelred forced out of the population with a hated tax – the *Danegeld*. The Vikings saw England as a soft touch and invaded, taking the crown. England now had a Danish king. Alfred the Great must have turned in his grave.

But it was not bad news for everyone. There were many people of Scandinavian blood in northern and eastern England from the days of the Danelaw, and the Danish King Cnut, who came to the throne in 1016, was a strong and intelligent king. One of the many reforms he made was to reduce the number of earldoms in England and make them bigger, and he gave one of the greatest of them – Wessex – to a young Englishman who had impressed him with his bravery; a Saxon called Godwin – Harold's father.

When Ethelred died Cnut had married his widow, Emma. Emma was a Norman, and her two sons by Ethelred – Alfred and Edward – were in exile in Normandy under the protection of her father, Duke Richard. Cnut already had a son by an English wife – a son called Harold Harefoot – and now he had another – Harthacnut – by Emma. But too many heirs can be as big a problem as too few. With all these sons, there was bound to be trouble.

Sure enough, when Cnut died there was a vicious scramble for power among his four sons. Harold

Harefoot held the throne first but died three years after he was crowned. Harthacnut grabbed it next, but he only lasted two years, dropping dead during a heavy drinking session. Alfred had been murdered, probably by Harold Harefoot, and so the half-Norman Edward, as the sole survivor, finally sat on the English throne.

Edward may have been related to Alfred the Great, but he was no more a fighting man than his father, Ethelred, had been. Edward was pious and unworldly, more suited to being an abbot than a king, and he became known as Edward the Confessor. Pious or not, he could also be paranoid, petty and cruel, particularly where the Godwin family was concerned.

There was no love lost whatsoever between Edward the Confessor and Earl Godwin. Not only had Godwin been raised to his high status by the hated King Cnut, he had also married into the Danish royal family making him seem, in Edward's mind, to have a divided loyalty.

And, just as Edward distrusted Godwin and his half-Danish children, Godwin was highly suspicious of the half-Norman Edward's French and Norman favourites at court. These included the King's nephew, Earl Ralph, who had an earldom near Wales, and the King's brother-in-law, Eustace of Boulogne.

But worse still, Edward strongly suspected Godwin of having a hand in the murder of his brother, Alfred. Edward and Alfred had made a botched bid to reclaim the English crown. It went horribly wrong, and though Edward escaped, Alfred was captured, blinded and left to die a slow and painful death. Edward had good reason to believe that even if Godwin had not done the deed himself, he had at least handed Alfred over to his killers. How Edward must have hated him.

Despite this, not only did Godwin keep his earldom when Edward became king, but Edward had the sense to see how useful a man like Godwin could be. Besides, Edward was no warrior. The last thing he wanted was a confrontation with Godwin. Not yet anyway. In fact Edward made Godwin even more powerful by marrying his daughter, Edith, in 1045.

Queen Edith was clever – she spoke several languages – and she was beautiful, too. But royal marriages are about producing heirs to the throne – and in those terms the marriage was a failure. Edward seems to have looked on Edith as more like a daughter than a wife.

Godwin and his Danish wife had no such problem. As well as Edith, they had another daughter, Gunnhildre, and six sons, Harold being one of them, born some time around 1024. Godwin's daughter was married to the King and between them, Godwin, his sons and his nephew controlled four of the seven earldoms, which amounted to most of England south of the River Humber. Harold was part of the most powerful family in England but the Godwinson brothers would be a mixed blessing to their father – and to England.

Harold was not the eldest son. Svein Godwinson was the son who ran things for Godwin when he was away. But Godwin was a powerful and ambitious man, and men like that can drive their sons too hard. Maybe this explains the crazed character of Harold's elder brother.

Svein was always wild, but in 1046 he kidnapped an abbess, a crime that was shocking even by the standards of the eleventh century. King Edward had no choice but to exile him, and in any case he was more than happy to punish a Godwinson. But Svein's behaviour only worsened. He broke the terms of his exile and returned, kidnapping his Danish cousin, Bjorn – a member of the Danish royal family and one of the earls of England – and murdered him in cold blood.

This latest outrage gave the King another opportunity to humiliate the Godwin clan. He declared Svein Godwinson *nithing* – a creature so low that anyone was legally permitted to kill him on sight without fear of being punished. Svein was eventually said to have taken himself on a pilgrimage to the Holy Land as penance for his many sins, dying on the way back in Constantinople (present-day Istanbul).

Harold's family had suffered a huge setback and it gave new confidence to another powerful faction in England – the King's French and Norman favourites that the Godwinson clan hated so much. The two sides were set on a collision course.

Sure enough, in 1051 Edward's brother-in-law, Eustace of Boulogne, sparked off a fight that was going to have serious consequences for Harold and his family. Eustace and his men lorded themselves round Dover, bullying the locals, and ended up being attacked by an angry mob.

The French were outnumbered but they were armed and well trained. There were fatalities on both sides.

Eustace went to the King and demanded that Dover be punished. Dover was under Godwin's protection and there was no way that he was going to take Eustace's side and ride against his own countrymen. He refused a direct order from the King, and that was something no one, however powerful, was allowed to do.

King Edward summoned his court to meet at Gloucester and the men of the *witangemot* discussed the case. The Norman Archbishop of Canterbury, Robert of Jumièges, and Edward's other foreign favourites seized their chance to get rid of the troublesome Godwin family for good.

Harold's family were not very popular among the other earls of England – they were far too powerful for their liking. So the Normans swung the *witangemot* in favour of demanding that Godwin appear before the King in London to explain himself. This would also give Edward the opportunity to finally bring Godwin to justice for the killing of his brother, Alfred.

Harold's father could see where all this was heading and he tried to raise an army, but even among their friends, no one had the stomach for a civil war. Whatever people thought of Eustace of Boulogne, an order from the King could not be ignored. Loyalty was everything.

Now Harold and his family were outlawed, just as Svein had been. How Edward must have enjoyed seeing the Godwin clan forced to flee into exile, just as he had had to do when the Danes took over.

Harold and his younger brother, Leofwine, went to Ireland, while his father and the rest of the family went to Flanders, the same country that had taken in Svein when he was exiled. Edward had to make do with the Godwins he could get his hands on. Queen Edith was spitefully stripped of her royal privileges and packed off to a nunnery, and Harold's youngest brother, Wulfnoth, and his nephew, Hakon, were taken hostage and sent to Normandy. The Godwinson earldoms and land were confiscated, and handed over to the likes of Archbishop Robert. Harold Godwinson's story might have ended there.

But the Godwin clan was not about to be beaten quite so easily. They had lost their titles and land, but they were still very rich and had supporters willing to help them. Godwin arranged for funds to be sent to Harold and Leofwine in Ireland, where they recruited Norse-Irish mercenaries and hired ships. Godwin hired even more ships in Bruges, including the crews to man them. Within a year they returned, armed to the teeth and ready to fight.

Harold and Leofwine came from the west at the head of an armed force. They landed at Porlock in Somerset but were beaten back by Edward's men and had to sail on. Harold took his ships all the way round Cornwall and then headed east to be reunited with his father and his fleet at the Isle of Wight in August. From there, the combined Godwin force sailed along the south coast, heading for London.

Harold and his family were heroes to the people of Kent and Sussex, and they were cheered on their way as they stopped every now and then to pick up supporters. By the time they reached the Thames estuary they were more than a match for the force that Edward had gathered to meet them.

Although the Godwin clan may not have been popular with all Englishmen, no one was going to have a civil war to help Edward's Norman favourites. The northern earls, Leofric of Mercia and Siward of Northumbria, made it clear that this was not their fight. Edward was furious, but there was nothing he could do. Half of his earls – the Godwin family – were about to attack him; the rest – except for his Norman nephew, Earl Ralph – were refusing to support him. Robert of Jumièges and the Norman bishops of Worcester and London fled for their lives. Edward had no option but to cave in and accept the Godwin family back.

On 15 September 1052 another *witangemot* was called and this time things went very differently. Edward was forced to overturn the outlaw status he had placed on Harold's family, clear their names and restore their lands and privileges. Edith was brought out of her nunnery and was Queen once more. Robert of Jumièges was replaced as Archbishop of Canterbury with the man who would eventually give King Edward the last rites – Stigand.

It was a total humiliation for Edward, but Harold's father did not have long to enjoy it. In April 1053 he keeled over suddenly after feasting with the King. Harold and his brothers carried him out of the hall. It may have been a stroke or a heart attack; it may even have been poison – we do not know – but in a few days he was dead. Harold Godwinson was now Earl of Wessex.

Just as he had relied on Godwin, and despite his personal feelings for him, Edward the Confessor quickly came to rely on his *new* Earl of Wessex. The weak and unworldly Edward needed a military leader, and Harold was just the man for the job. He had been brought up as a warrior, but he was far more than that. He was intelligent enough to see that war was not always the answer to every problem.

The Celts of Wales and the Anglo-Saxons had always been at each other's throats, but when trouble flared up again, Harold was wise enough to see an opportunity to make peace with the Celts. Harold managed to get the Welsh King, Gruffydd ap Llewellyn, and the very reluctant Edward together to make peace on the banks of the River Severn.

It did not last, though. In 1062 Harold the peacemaker became Harold the warrior when the Welsh began raiding again and Edward ordered him to retaliate. Straight away he showed his skill as a soldier with a grasp of the importance of surprise in combat. He threw caution to the wind and crossed over the border, riding straight into the white teeth of winter.

It was the last thing the Welsh were expecting. Gruffydd ap Llewellyn only just managed to escape with his life, and Harold burned the Welsh fleet before heading back through the snow into England and to his King at court in Gloucester.

But Harold had not finished with the Welsh. In the spring of 1063 he struck again, sailing from Bristol and leaving a trail of destruction through Wales. Harold and his men were brutal; anyone who even *looked* as if they were getting in their way was hacked down and, finally, the Welsh could take no more. In desperation they turned on Gruffydd, killing him themselves and bringing back his severed head to Harold as proof. Harold, in turn, sent the Welsh leader's head to Edward to show him that the job was done.

Harold's defeat of the Welsh made him famous beyond the shores of England. Foreigners began to refer to him as *"Dux Anglorum"* – Duke of the English. He was called a *"sub-regulus"* – an under-king, and that is what Harold was, in effect. He was certainly the most important man beside the king.

Harold was Edward's military commander, but he was more than that. Harold was also a skilful politician. He was Edward's ambassador and travelled abroad as his representative. He visited Flanders. He met Pope Victor II in Cologne.

Meanwhile, Edward still showed no sign of producing an heir to the throne and decided that a man called Edward the Exile would be the best choice to succeed him. Most people, including Harold, seemed to agree. Edward the Exile was the grandson of Ethelred the

Unready, but on the side from Ethelred's English wife, Aelgifu, not the Norman Emma. The absence of Norman blood might explain why the Godwinsons were happy to support him.

Cnut had sent the infant Edward to Sweden to be disposed of when he took the English crown, but instead of murdering the child, the King of Sweden sent him to Hungary where he had lived ever since. Now Edward the Confessor invited him back to England.

Edward the Exile arrived in 1057 just as planned, but no sooner had he landed than he mysteriously dropped dead. He never even got to see the King. It seems very likely that he was killed, but by whom? Like so many other details in this story there are claims and counter claims. The Normans believed that Harold killed Edward the Exile, to leave the way open for himself to be king. Whatever the truth, Harold was looking like a king already. And that certainly did not make Edward trust or like him any better.

The only Godwinson that the King had any time for at all, apart from his wife, was Harold's brother, Tostig. He had fought beside Harold in his campaign against the Welsh. Tostig was a real favourite of the King and under normal circumstances should really have been at the King's side as he lay dying, but as we have seen, he was not. In fact not only was he not in the room; he was not even in the country. And worse than that, he was now Harold's sworn enemy. But why?

The trouble had begun when Tostig became Earl of Northumbria in 1055, increasing the Godwinson hold over England even further. The clan was so powerful they made sure Tostig got the earldom when Earl Siward died, against Northumbrian wishes. Northumbria, like Wessex and Mercia, had once been a kingdom, and there was still a feeling of it being a separate country with its own national identity. It had been part of the Danelaw – the area occupied by the Danish invaders with whom Alfred the Great had done battle, and then occupied by the Norse. There were many people of Scandinavian descent. Things were done differently there; and it was a wild and dangerous place.

Tostig had none of Harold's charm; in fact Tostig rubbed people up the wrong way. He was stiff and pompous. He was determined to teach these lawless Northumbrians a lesson, and set about knocking them into shape. It did not go down very well with the locals. And to make matters worse, half the time Tostig was not even in the earldom; he was way down south enjoying himself being the King's favourite. Edward was no more popular with the Northumbrians than Tostig was – he had never seen fit to visit them in his entire reign.

In October 1065, on one of Tostig's long trips south, the Northumbrians rebelled, killing Tostig's men. Harold was said to be out hunting with Tostig in Wiltshire when they heard the news. Harold must have had mixed feelings. The Northumbrians were a troublesome lot, but he knew his brother, too. Whoever was at fault, this meant big trouble. It could mean that England might start coming apart at the seams in a bloody civil war.

Tostig ran to the King and Edward was outraged. How dare the Northumbrians behave like this towards a favourite of the King? He demanded that an army be sent to crush the rebels, but the *witangemot* saw things differently. They said that Tostig had brought the trouble on his own head and Harold tended to agree.

Tostig went berserk. How dare Harold go against him? His own brother? He even accused Harold of stirring things up against him, though Harold swore that this was nonsense. Why would he? Harold tried to get the two sides to agree, but it came to nothing.

As the King's general, Harold went to meet the rebels and told them to lay down their arms. The rebels told *him* that they would not take back Tostig whatever happened and they had chosen a different earl. His name was Morcar, and he was the teenage grandson of Earl Leofric of Mercia and Godifu (otherwise known as Lady Godiva). Alongside his brother Edwin, the Earl of Mercia, Morcar threatened to march on London and take the matter up with the King in person.

Edward demanded Harold mobilize an army to attack the northern rebels, but no one answered the call to arms. It was yet another humiliation for the King, but another sign that the English understood the need to avoid civil war. They would not fight a civil war to defend the King's Norman favourites and they certainly were not going to fight one to support Tostig Godwinson.

In the end, Edward was forced to exile Tostig. It must have been a final blow to the old man at the end of a life full of bitterness and disappointment, much of it involving the Godwin family. Perhaps it even contributed to the illness that finally killed him.

But it says something about this weak king, though, that at the end, Edward could put aside his feud with the Godwin clan. He could see that whatever his differences were with Harold Godwinson; he really was the best man to protect England.

And England *was* going to need protecting.

William
Duke of Normandy
January 1066

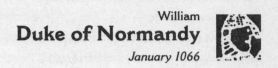

THEY SAY THAT bad news travels fast. Duke William of Normandy was just setting out on a hunt near his capital at Rouen when an English messenger arrived, saying, *"King Edward is dead, and Harold is raised to the kingdom."*

The hunt was called off. William was not a man to show emotion, good or bad, but retreated into a frightening silence that no one dared interrupt. He is said to have stormed off, got in a boat, rowed across to his palace and sat on his own, leaning with his face pressed against a stone column, his cloak pulled over his head.

William seemed to have gone into shock. He might have stayed like that all day had not his right-hand man, William fitzOsbern, arrived and told him to pull himself together. There was no time to grieve. He needed to act.

William was distantly – very distantly – related to

Edward the Confessor; William's grandfather's sister was Edward's mother. But William was not "grieving" for Edward, but for himself. In fact "sulking" would be a better word for it.

It was not the news of Edward's death that had upset him; it was the news of Harold's coronation. William wanted the English crown for himself. But why would this foreigner think he deserved to be King of England? To answer that question, we need to look into the past; into the history of Normandy and its links with England.

Just like England, the French coast had suffered at the murderous hands of the Vikings. In fact, Normandy had been created in 911 when the French King – Charles the Simple – had given lands to a Viking called Rollo, or Rolf, in the hope that he would act as a guard dog against other Viking raiders. William was descended from this Viking stock.

France did not exist as we know it today. The Franks were one of the peoples who prospered – like the Anglo-Saxons – after the fall of the Roman Empire. The Frankish – French – kings were based in an area centred on Paris and ruled the surrounding principalities, whose leaders swore allegiance to them. Rollo could stay as long as he swore allegiance to Charles and converted to Christianity. Rollo agreed.

These *Duces Northmannorum* (dukes of the Northmen) settled but proved to be aggressive neighbours, greedily extending their frontiers. And they were not much better *within* their borders, as they schemed and murdered in endless power struggles.

Normandy was to become more and more French – the Normans now spoke French and dressed like Franks. Normandy also became more and more powerful until in 1002, Duke Richard – William's great-grandfather – was taken seriously enough that he could marry his daughter, Emma, to the King of England, Ethelred the Unready.

In a way it was ironic that the English Ethelred chose the descendant of Vikings for his bride, because as we have seen Vikings were wrecking his country and would eventually invade and take his throne, forcing him to flee to Normandy for protection.

When Ethelred died, the Normans were delighted when the Danish King Cnut took Ethelred's Norman widow as his wife. Emma already had two sons by Ethelred – Alfred and Edward – at the Norman court and now she had a son – Harthacnut – with Cnut. Whatever happened, it seemed likely that there would soon be an English king with Norman blood in his veins. The Normans waited patiently.

In 1027 or 1028, William was born, the illegitimate son of the ill-tempered Robert I, Duke of Normandy (Robert the Devil as he was called, with good reason) and Herleve, the daughter of a tanner (leather worker) at the Norman court. Illegitimacy does not seem to have carried the stigma it was to have later in history, but it was noted enough for William to be called William the Bastard in his own lifetime.

Then in 1035 Cnut the Great and Robert the Devil both died. Eventually, as we have seen, the half-Norman Edward became King of England, while in Normandy the eight-year-old William became Duke of a country that was seething with violent in-fighting. He probably went to see Henry of France to swear allegiance. But William's chances of survival were very slim.

In fact William's chances would have been nil, had not Robert the Devil left him in the charge of some tough and clever men. William was schooled by a monk called Ralph Moine, sharing his classes with William fitzOsbern, Roger of Montgomery and Roger of Beaumont. Along with his half-brothers, Odo and Robert, these classmates would be at William's side for years to come.

William was no scholar; he may even have been illiterate. But his real passion was for war. He learned about castle-building and became an expert in the sword and the lance, riding well from an early age. He had a talent for warfare – and he was going to need it.

One by one, his guardians were bumped off; one of them having his throat cut in the boy William's bedroom as he slept. Norman nobles had built scores of castles and were competing with each other for power. It only seemed a matter of time before Normandy would fall apart. When the squabbling Norman nobles openly rebelled against William, trying to ambush and murder him, the 19-year-old Duke of Normandy went to King Henry of France for help. The ties of loyalty ran both ways. William had an obligation of loyalty to Henry if he was called upon, and Henry, as William's lord, had a duty to protect William.

So, in 1047, the 21-year-old William faced his first battle, at the head of a small contingent of Normans in a French force led by Henry. It was the Battle of Val-es-Dunes and, like most battles, it was a chaotic mess. William could easily have been killed. But he was not.

In fact William not only survived, but he fought bravely and, most importantly, he was on the winning side. William may even have personally killed one of the rebel's champions; a man with the intimidating name of Harder of Bayeux. The Norman rebels had fought ferociously, but they were just as ferociously slaughtered when they were driven headlong into the River Orne. Weighed down by heavy coats of mail, many simply drowned in the river. Those who did not drown were stabbed and hacked to death by Henry and William's men. The river ran red with blood, and corpses, stripped of their armour, floated downstream.

Not only was William showing his capacity for bravery and leadership, he was also beginning to show his capacity for cruelty. At 25, he led a successful campaign against Anjou. During a siege of the town of Alençon, the inhabitants made the mistake of banging on sheets of leather and shouting, *"Hides! Hides for the tanner!"* in a goading reference to William's mother who was a tanner's daughter.

Whether William was sensitive about his illegitimacy or his mother's low birth, the Alençons certainly lived to regret it. He had the hands and feet of 31 of its townsfolk chopped off for their impudence.

In 1050 or 1053 William married Matilda, daughter of Baldwin V of Flanders. Together they had four sons and six daughters and unlike many of the nobility of eleventh-century Europe, they seemed to have been completely devoted to each other. But that did not mean that William was going soft.

The Duke was an intimidating man even at this young age. King Henry of France was already beginning to wonder if it had been such a good idea to help him. Maybe it was time to remind this young upstart who was the real boss. When another rebellion started in Normandy, instead of coming to William's aid, Henry invaded Normandy allied with the counts of Anjou and Ponthieu.

But Henry's invasion went horribly wrong, from the French point of view. The force was split into three prongs, and the prong led by Count Enguerrand of Ponthieu was hammered by William and the Count was killed. Henry was forced to retreat.

In 1054 Henry came back, bent on revenge for his humiliation the year before. His forces left a trail of destruction as they went, and when they arrived at the town of Mortimer they went on the rampage in a frenzy of looting, murdering and raping all through the night.

Just as dawn arrived, fires began to erupt all over the town. The French panicked and ran to escape. They found every street and alleyway blocked by William's men, armed to the teeth, firelight flickering along their sword blades. The French were slaughtered and Henry was forced to retreat again.

In 1057 Henry of France and the Count of Anjou tried again. Third time lucky, maybe. Sure enough, this time things seemed to go better, but only because William refused to meet them in battle. Then, as they were returning home loaded down with booty, William hit them as they crossed the River Dives.

Henry was safely on the other side of the river and could do nothing but watch as his men were cut to pieces, unable to send men to their aid because of the rising tide. He had wanted to show who was boss and he had. It was William.

In 1060, Henry of France died, leaving his eight-year-old son under the guardianship of William's father-in-law. Anjou descended into civil war following the death of its count, Geoffrey Martel. William had no one to stop him now, and he attacked Maine to the south and brought it under Norman control for a while. He planned a campaign against the Celts of Brittany to the west. And he started to look north, across the Channel, to England.

It is possible that the childless King of England, who had spent his childhood in the Norman court and whose mother was herself Norman, might have given William to understand that he was his choice to succeed him. Some even claimed that William had visited England and had heard the promise from Edward's own lips – but the dithering Edward might have given that idea to others as well, including the wayward Tostig Godwinson. In any case it was very unlikely that the *witangemot* would have supported the Norman William as heir.

Then, in 1064 a messenger came from across Normandy's eastern border, from Ponthieu. The message concerned a prisoner that Count Guy had recently captured and placed in his dungeons. William immediately sent a message to Guy. Hand over the prisoner, or else.

Now Guy knew all about William and knew that he was not a man to cross. As Count of Ponthieu he had answered the call to arms and joined Henry I's raid into Normandy, and spent two years in William's dungeons for his troubles. He did not want to repeat the experience.

William rode to meet Guy and his prisoner at a prearranged rendezvous point, and for doing as he was told, Guy was rewarded with money to cover any ransom he might have claimed and given a manor. That was William's way; rewards for those who obeyed, swift and brutal punishment for those who did not.

And now William took charge of Guy's prisoner. The two men whose lives later crashed together with such force came face to face for the first time. The prisoner was none other than Harold Godwinson.

But what on earth was Harold Godwinson doing on this side of the Channel? The answer to that question was argued about for many years after and is *still* argued about. Some say that he was on a hunting expedition along the south coast from his manor in Bosham, near Chichester – the Bayeux Tapestry shows him setting out with dogs and hawks – but got blown off course. This is not nearly as crazy as it sounds. Although Ponthieu is a hundred miles away from Chichester, the ships of this era were not very manoeuvrable. Once out at sea, even experienced sailors were at the mercy of the winds, and if a gale blew up heading for Ponthieu that was where the ship would end up, like it or not.

But that is only one possible explanation. When Edward the Confessor sent Harold's family into exile, he kept a couple of the Godwin family members as hostages. Harold's brother, Wulfnoth, and his nephew, Hakon, were sent to William for safe-keeping and were still in Normandy. One possible explanation is that Harold was going to ask William to return his relatives.

Yet another explanation is that Edward had sent Harold to Normandy as his envoy, specifically to offer William the crown when he died. Again, this is not impossible. Harold had acted as an ambassador for Edward before, although it is difficult to imagine the passionately English Harold meekly agreeing to offer a Norman the English crown, especially as he was so powerful at home.

Whatever the true story, Harold would certainly not have been intending to land in Ponthieu, which was an infamous haunt of wreckers and kidnappers. William seems to have treated Harold well when they got back to Normandy. He took him back to Rouen, where he was guest of honour at a great feast and tournament. William introduced him to his children and Harold seems to have got on very well with William's wife, Matilda.

William told Harold that he was planning an attack on Conan, the leader of the Celts to the west of Normandy, in Brittany. Harold was famous for his victories against the Celts of Wales and William asked that he come along. Perhaps he even asked the Englishman for some tips.

And if William was trying to see at first hand what he would be up against if he and Harold ever met in battle, he must have been impressed. The Bayeux Tapestry shows some Norman soldiers getting trapped in quicksand near Mont St Michel. Harold is pictured coming to their rescue, pulling them out single-handedly by brute strength.

After a month or so of chasing the Breton Celts, William and Harold quit the campaign and returned to Normandy. William was quick to acknowledge Harold's part in the campaign in Brittany. Some say that William knighted him, but if he had, Harold would have had to recognize William as his lord, and again it is difficult to imagine Harold doing that.

But it is what happened – or did not happen – when William and Harold returned to Normandy that made all the difference in the months to come. According to William and the Normans, Harold made an oath – at Bayeux, or Bonneville-sur-Tourqes or Rouen; a sacred oath sworn on holy relics. We can't know if he did, but perhaps it is more important what people *believe* was done; sometimes that is more important than the truth. And the Normans said that Harold had sworn to support William's claim to the throne and even to be his representative in England. We live in a time when the idea of a political leader breaking a promise is not shocking, but in 1066, there where not many things a man could do that were worse than breaking a sacred oath. Whatever the truth of the Norman version of events, Harold was allowed to return to England, and was even allowed to take his nephew Hakon with him. Harold's little brother Wulfnoth, however, would remain William's prisoner in Normandy.

When Edward the Confessor died, William called a meeting of all his top men. He told them that he intended to invade England, to conquer it and to take the crown. They in turn advised calling a council of all the Norman nobles where they said they would publicly back his plans.

But when a full council of nobles did eventually take place at Lillebonne, the mood was not nearly as enthusiastic as it had been with William's elite. It seems not to have occurred to William that there would be any serious objection and he was furious. William was not the kind of man who was used to hearing the word "no".

The English were too powerful, the nobles said. There was not enough money to pay for the soldiers and ships needed, they said. William dissolved the meeting and went to work on the council members, one by one. He tempted some with talk of the fortunes that were there for the taking when they landed in England; the land and the loot. And if their greed was not enough, William used threats. William knew how to intimidate people; you were either for him or against him, it was as simple as that.

The barons said that their obligation to William did not extend to serving overseas and they probably had a point. They were not defending Normandy after all; they were invading another country. But they were also terrified of crossing the Channel, and they were right to be. The crossing was unpredictable at the best of times, and they would have to transport thousands of men, horses and equipment.

But however much they feared the sea, they feared William more. One by one they caved in, eventually agreeing to provide double the amount of knights they had been obliged to provide under their bond of loyalty. William must have secretly hoped that they were made of sterner stuff when it came to the fight with the English.

William wanted everyone to know that he was in the right; that he was only after justice. He needed to make the invasion more than personal, more than just about his desire to be King of England. And this is where a Norman prior called Lanfranc came in.

Lanfranc helped William to devise a way to get the

Pope on board. He sent an envoy to Pope Alexander II in Rome, saying that if William became King of England, they could reform the English Church, rein it in and cure it of its peculiarities – like its habit of writing things down in English instead of Latin.

Although, just a hundred years ago, William's Viking ancestors robbed monasteries and murdered priests, William was an enthusiastic supporter of the Church and of the monastery system. William paid for huge monasteries to be built and endowed them with money. Much of this was booty from his military campaigns but the monks did not seem to mind. The monks in their turn would pray for William's soul; for the forgiveness of his sins. They were power stations of prayer, working day and night for their benefactor's salvation.

Lanfranc's envoy told the Pope that Harold Godwinson was a liar; a perjurer; that he had made, and broken, a sacred oath, sworn on holy relics – an oath supporting William's claim to the English throne. Now, while King Edward's funeral feast was barely cold, Harold had seized the crown for himself.

Pope Alexander II was being asked to decide whose claim was the more righteous and he gave his blessing to William. He gave the Duke a papal banner to carry and a ring, supposedly containing a hair of St Peter's, which William would wear round his neck in battle. Those relics were weapons; more powerful than a thousand spears. They elevated William's personal ambitions to the status of crusade, of holy war.

In fact the Normans were in the front line in the "holy" war against Islam in the Holy Land and Spain. Now, here in the north, they would be soldiers of Christ, too. And if there was land to be seized and treasure to be looted, well that would be a bonus. Men from all over Europe flocked to the holy cause.

Harold
The Long-haired Star
Spring – Summer 1066

AT EASTER, THE MEMBERS of the *witangemot* were back in London, attending King Harold's Easter Court at Edward's palace on Thorney Island at Westminster. Easter was one of the biggest feast days of the year, coming after the fast of Lent.

The English liked a feast, and as this was the King's hall, this one would have been quite something. Meat would have been roasting on spits over glowing fires; fires that flickered across the brooches and knife blades of the king's noblemen. Servants would have gone round the long tables, bringing the diners their roast beef, chicken, duck, goose or pigeon. As this was a feast fit for a king, there would have been venison, too. There would have been no roast potatoes with all this meat, though; they would not be brought back to England for hundreds of years. The same goes for tomatoes, chocolate, tea, coffee and sugar. Honey was the only sweetener in 1066. There would have been bread – but unleavened; more like Indian nan bread or Greek pitta.

Harold and his fellow diners would have been a messy and rowdy lot by our standards. There were no forks and they carried their own all-purpose knife called a *seaxe* with them to cut their food – a knife that was also used to hunt and to fight with. *Seaxes* may have given Saxons their name.

Harold was in his element here. He was likeable, relaxed, quick-witted and good-humoured – at least among friends. Maybe the love of Harold's life was here – Edith Swan-neck. There is no record that Harold and Edith were ever married, but they were together for many years, and had several children together.

Harold couldn't have been more different from up-tight Edward the Confessor. Drinking-horn in hand, he would have listened along with the other diners to the minstrels reciting the heroic poems that warriors loved to hear at times like this; very long poems telling stirring tales of heroes and monsters, warriors and battles, real and mythical.

One of these poems may have been *Beowulf*, with its tale of a terrible monster called Grendel who rose up from the marshes to kill warriors sleeping on the benches in their lord's hall. Or they could have listened to *The Battle of Maldon*, about a doomed English stand against Viking invaders, with its vision of the warrior's code of honour:

I swear that from this spot not one foot's space
Of ground shall I give up. I shall go onwards,
In the fight to avenge my friend and lord.
My deeds shall give no warrant for words of blame
To steadfast men on Stour, now he is stretched lifeless
– That I left the battlefield a lordless man,
Turned from home. The irons shall take me
Point or edge...

In the fireglow of the King's hall, Harold and the other listeners knew that one day *their* loyalty and courage would be tested. And it might be soon. Trouble was brewing and everyone in that room knew it.

At the end of April, a couple of nights after Easter, there was a terrifying sign that disaster might be about to strike the English. A weird *"long-haired star"* appeared in the night sky; a star that seemed to have a tail of glowing white fire. We know it now as Halley's Comet and it was making its usual 76-yearly appearance, but to the superstitious people of 1066 it was a supernatural omen; its fiery tail was a warning of the actual fires that would follow below it, in its wake.

Harold stood with members of the *witangemot* outside Edward's palace at Westminster, surrounded by the brambles that gave Thorney Island its name, the sky ink-black above the marshes. What did *he* make of this sign? If Harold was the oath-breaker that William said he was, then it may indeed have seemed like a terrible sign from God. But on the other hand, even if Harold *did* make that oath to support William's claim to the throne, he could not have known at the time that Edward was going to die and name him as his successor. After all, if Edward had lived longer, then young Edgar the Aetheling might have been a stronger contender. Harold may have had no reason to feel guilty at all.

Harold had not *seized* the crown, whatever the Normans might have said. Maybe William had misjudged the situation and not realized that Harold was even in the running for the throne when he had him in his grasp. Perhaps that explains William's reaction at the news. He was furious with himself for making such a terrible mistake by letting Harold go.

It was clear, though, that William was not going to take the news lying down and that Harold had to expect the worst. The only coins that Harold produced in his reign had one word on the back instead of the usual cross. It said *pax* – peace – but it can only have been wishful thinking.

No sooner had the comet disappeared from English skies than its powers as an evil omen seemed to be proved. That May, shiploads of armed men attacked the Isle of Wight, strutted around for a while, fleeced the inhabitants and left, harassing the coast as they sailed eastward, eventually anchoring at Sandwich, in Kent. But it wasn't William; it was Harold's bitter and revenge-hungry brother, Tostig Godwinson.

Kent was under the protection of another of Harold's brothers, Leofwine Godwinson, but Harold took command himself and headed down to the Kent coast with men at arms. Tostig was hardly going to wait around, and he sailed on to Thanet, where he met up with Copsig, his old deputy from his days as Earl of Northumbria, recently arrived with more men from Orkney. From there they headed off into the North Sea and the east coast, recruiting sailors on route, and entered the Humber with a fleet of 60 ships. He was a force to be reckoned with, and he seemed almost crazy with his desire to hit back at Harold. But this only made Tostig careless.

Tostig and his raiding party attacked Lindsey in his old earldom of Northumbria. But the northern earls, Morcar of Northumbria and Edwin of Mercia, arrived to defend the country. It had been they who had led the revolt against Tostig in the first place. How they must have enjoyed the chance to lead an attack against him, and how humiliating it must have been for Tostig to be beaten back by the men who had forced his exile.

In the face of armed opposition, Tostig's new recruits deserted in droves and his once impressive fleet wilted to a mere 12 ships. He scuttled north, seeking refuge with Malcolm of Scotland. England had faced its first test well.

It was said that Harold may have agreed to marry Morcar and Edwin's sister at the Christmas Court, although this is by no means certain. If he *had* then the deal seemed to have paid off. Morcar and Edwin could rarely be counted on, but this time they had pulled their weight – though more out of a personal grudge against Tostig than for the good of England.

But Harold knew that this was unlikely to be the worst of it. He decided that Tostig's raid on the south coast might just be the start of a full-blown Norman invasion. What was certain was that he needed men to counter the threat, whether from Tostig or William, or both. It was time to mobilize the *fyrd*.

The *fyrd* had begun under Alfred the Great as a way of trying to deal with the invading Danish army. It was a kind of militia requiring landowners to provide armed men for military service in defence of the realm; a kind of conscription of all able-bodied men between the ages of 15 and 54.

This was a sophisticated call-up system for the army, where the raising of men was based on how much land was held and worked because of the rule of loyalty and duty, which ran all the way from the lowest peasant to the king – and back again. *Ceorls* (churls) were free peasants who worked the land. A *ceorl* did not own much land, and the land he held, he had been granted by a *thegn* (thane). A *thegn* would hold much more land than a *ceorl* and with this extra wealth came extra responsibility. It was a minimum requirement of a *thegn* that he provide one armed man and the money to keep him for two months. The more land he owned, the more men he would have to supply, and the men of a wealthy *thegn* would probably train and fight together as a unit. A *thegn* held his land from an earl or monastery, often as a gift or reward for loyalty. Above the *thegn*, was the earl and he held his land from the king. The king held his land from God, or at least it was believed he held it by "God's grace".

Everyone was bound together by a bond of duty and obligation. The *ceorl* had an obligation of loyalty to the *thegn*, the *thegn* to the earl, the earl to the king and all the way back again. If the king called, the earls came running, trailing everyone else in their wake. It was a two-way street. Those at the top expected loyalty from those below them, those at the bottom expected protection from those above them.

In the summer of 1066, Harold's new army made its way to the mustering points – pre-arranged meeting-places – walking and riding along Roman roads and ancient trackways, through fields and meadows, with May blossom on the hawthorn trees and cuckoos calling in the woods.

The farmers turned-soldiers wore their own clothes – it would be centuries before soldiers would wear a uniform. They trudged along in the standard woollen tunic that all men in northern Europe wore at the time. It was belted at the waist, with trouser-like leggings underneath and strips of material wrapped round the calves for extra protection – against brambles for one thing. On their feet, they wore leather shoes or boots.

They wore knee-length cloaks pinned at the right shoulder or neck by a brooch and some may have worn felt or leather caps. They wore their hair long, and many had enormous moustaches. Some would have worn jewellery – necklaces or armbands. Some may have had tattoos.

Many of Harold's soldiers would never have strayed further than the fields around their own villages. As they approached the muster points, these young farmers now stared wide-eyed at a scene that must have seemed straight out of a poem. From far and wide men answered the call to arms and it must have been quite a sight as the *thegns* tried to organize the new arrivals.

As the men of the *fyrd* joined their comrades, the air would have been filled with the noise of men testing their weapons and shouting to friends. Few would have ever seen a gathering of so many men. Some may even have been lucky enough to have seen their new king.

Spears were by far the most common weapons at that time – they were a cheap and familiar weapon to most men, and would have been used in hunting. They consisted of a long ash-wood pole tipped by an iron blade; barbed (hooked) blades were used for throwing and leaf-shaped ones for thrusting.

Another hunting weapon was the bow. Bows were of the longbow type, made of ash or yew and standing about two-metres high. The bowstrings were made of linen thread and the arrows were made of poplar wood. No doubt men who were skilful with the bow would have brought one along to the muster point. In times to come, the English army would become famous for its archers, but in 1066 the English do not seem to have yet realized just how terrifying a weapon it could be, especially if used with a mass of longbowmen, all firing at one time. Perhaps they thought it was a cowardly weapon; that brave men fought face to face and did not kill from a distance.

Of course, Harold would have had the best weapons and the best armour money could buy, and the most sought-after weapon in the eleventh century was the sword. They were double-edged, designed for hacking and slashing rather than jabbing; and they were also *very* expensive. The sword had been the weapon of choice for centuries and sword-making was a highly prized and highly paid art, with craftsmen signing their work. Swords themselves were given names and were a symbol of honour. Ancient swords were treated like holy relics and carried into battle in the hope that they would bring victory to the owners.

Even a great warrior like Harold was not going to last long without some kind of protection from his opponents. Harold and his men wore two main pieces of armour – a conical helmet and a hauberk (a chain-mail smock). The Bayeux Tapestry shows Harold and his brothers, Gyrth and Leofwine, all wearing helmets with nose-guards and chain-mail hauberks. Like swords, hauberks were expensive and only people of fairly high status owned one.

Chain-mail was heavy, too – probably weighing about 14 kilograms – so you had to be strong just to wear a hauberk, but it was worth the effort for the protection it offered. Chain-mail was made up of interlocking loops of metal. It wouldn't stop an arrow or a lance, but it would deflect a sword blow, or at least turn what would have been fatal open wounds into survivable cracked ribs or broken bones. But the hauberk only covered the legs to the knees – and it did not cover the face. Soldiers were still astonishingly vulnerable.

There was another piece of protection – the shield. These were often round – although the Bayeux Tapestry also shows the English, and possibly Harold himself, holding kite-shaped ones. Shields were made of wooden planks, usually lime wood, and covered in painted cowhide with an iron boss, like the hub of a wheel, in the centre and an iron grip on the back to hold on to.

Shield bosses had become more and more conical over time. By 1066, they stuck out so much that they were a weapon in themselves, used to deliver a bone-jarring blow to an opponent. Shields could not stop swords or axes for ever, and the metal boss would often be the only bit left as the wood and hide around it was hacked off.

That summer, Harold rode surrounded by his bodyguards – the *huscarls*. *Huscarls* were introduced to England by the Danish kings of England and were full-time, well-equipped warriors, bound by an obligation of loyalty to lay down their lives if need be for their lord. Originally these men were all Scandinavians but by 1066 there were Englishmen serving in their ranks, and there were *huscarls* in the households of earls as well as of the king. These *huscarls* wielded the most frightening weapon in the English armoury: the battle-axe.

The battle-axe was a huge weapon, used originally in England by the Scandinavian invaders. It needed two hands to wield it and it struck terror into any opponent. The Bayeux Tapestry shows Harold's brother, Leofwine, using one. Harold and his brothers were half-Danish, of course, so they may well have been trained to use axes.

The English army had developed a tactic called the shield wall, with warriors standing in a line, overlapping their shields and inviting the enemy to attack. The men of the shield wall would jab their spears out at the enemy approach and occasionally part to allow a *huscarl* room to swing his battle-axe. It was simple and effective.

The strict code of loyalty displayed by the *huscarl* warrior elite would certainly be rewarded by gifts, but they may even have been paid a wage. Harold – along with every other ruler of the time – would also employ mercenaries; trained warriors who put their valuable expertise up for sale, and whose skill and experience could swing the outcome of a battle.

Despite the fact that their ancestors had been skilled horsemen, Harold and his men only seem to have used their horses to travel to the battle. Once the battle started they fought on foot. There seems to have even been a feeling that fighting on horseback was cowardly or unmanly. The English preferred to stand shoulder to shoulder and slug it out. In any case, English horses were short, stocky animals, suited to carrying heavy armour a long distance, but certainly not built for speed.

Harold also had a navy – vital for an island people who were always in danger from sea-borne invaders. In fact England had a naval tradition going back to King Alfred. This had been expanded by Ethelred and men were expected to serve at sea just as they were expected to serve in the army. England was not going to be a pushover for anybody. The men of the *fyrd* could afford to feel quietly confident. Harold had a fleet of 700 ships patrolling the south coast, watching and waiting for any sign of William's invasion force. He must have been reasonably confident that he could counter any move by the Normans.

In fact Harold's brother, Gyrth, who was Earl of East Anglia, was all for the English sailing to Normandy and attacking William before he was ready, instead of waiting around to see what he did next. Harold should have listened to the idea – it was a good one – but he dismissed it.

William carried on his preparations unchallenged.

William
Dives-sur-Mer
Spring – Summer 1066

AT THE END OF JULY 1066, William said farewell to his trusted queen, Matilda, and left her to reign in his absence. They seem to have been a genuinely devoted couple – if a rather odd-looking one; William was tall but Matilda was tiny – only a little over four-feet high. William met with his men at Dives-sur-Mer, near Caen, at the beginning of August.

His first problem in the spring of 1066 had been how to get his army to England in the first place. Unlike the English, the Normans did not have a navy to speak of. If they were going to get across the English Channel, William was going to have to build some ships. Out came the axes and down came the trees of Normandy.

We do not know how many ships were built or, for that matter, how many sailed. We do know that although Normans were descended from Vikings, their ships were smaller than the ocean-going Viking longships. They had a similar appearance, with one central mast and sail, but were smaller and broader, only about 12-metres long – more like fishing boats.

When William arrived on the coast, the flotilla for the invasion lay moored in the protection of an inland harbour awaiting his command to set sail. Also awaiting his commands was the army that had gathered to take part in the invasion.

The system of call-up in Normandy was not quite the same as in England, but it was similar. William's nobles had their own troops – household troops a little like the *huscarls* of England, bound to their lord, who was in turn bound to Duke William. Just as in England, William had given gifts of land and expected in return the absolute loyalty of the noble to whom he had given it. Nobles in their turn gave land to men they valued and paid their expenses, on the same basis – that when they were needed, they would come without question.

William looked out on a scene very similar to the one Harold witnessed on the other side of the Channel. The Normans used very similar weapons and their clothes and armour looked very much alike. In fact, all northern European warriors looked very similar, although the Normans, unlike the English and the Scandinavians, were clean-shaven and had very strange haircuts, shaving the back of their heads.

William's men wore conical helmets with nose-guards and chain-mail hauberks, sometimes with hoods of mail, or maybe even with leather hoods. Some sort of padded or quilted clothing may have been worn under the mail and padded-leather clothing may have been used instead of mail.

Norman shields were often kite-shaped and they had a system of leather straps rather than a simple iron bar to hold on to. The bosses on these shields were mostly decorative and the shields were often painted with animals and coloured patterns.

Swords were about 80 centimetres long, similar to the English, tapering slightly with a fairly short hilt (handle) and a rounded pommel at the end. The hilt was bound with leather strapping to give a good grip for one-handed sword-wielding. These swords might have had religious inscriptions etched into the blades or be marked by crosses. They might also have carried the maker's name. Just as with the English and Scandinavians, a sword's scabbard was wooden, wrapped in leather and preferably lined with wool (the natural oils would protect the sword blade and help stop it from rusting).

William used archers and may have seen the bow as being a much more important weapon than Harold did. He also employed an early form of crossbow. There was a lot less skill in firing a crossbow bolt than shooting an arrow, and that meant it was easier to train men to use them. It was certainly worth it, as a crossbow bolt was a deadly weapon.

Like all warriors at the time, the Normans used spears, for throwing and for thrusting. But there was one huge difference between the Normans and the English; Norman spears were by this time being carried by men on horseback – they were becoming lances. And this is the crucial difference between Harold and William; their differing attitudes to the horse. Although Harold's men had horses, could ride perfectly well and rode horses to battle, they fought as infantry (foot soldiers). William had cavalry (soldiers on horseback) and it helped to make the Normans an incredible fighting force, feared throughout the known world.

Cavalry meant speed and power of attack. A cavalryman had a height advantage over an infantryman and could use it to deliver blows with a lance, then follow it up with a secondary weapon such as a sword or a mace (metal club).

Lances were beginning to be used underarm or "couched". The weight and power of the horse increased the force of a lance, enabling cavalrymen to knock a rider from his horse or run a man through without any effort of their own. And as well as using their long lances underarm to skewer their opponents, cavalrymen could hurl them like javelins as they rode towards the enemy ranks.

The horse itself could also be a weapon. The Normans used specially bred war-horses, huge and heavily built. They needed to be able to carry an armed soldier, but be quick with it. All the war-horses were stallions, highly prized and very expensive. Norman nobles had their own stud farms, but the real experts in horse breeding were the monasteries, which gave William an added reason to be so encouraging to them.

These mounted Norman warriors called themselves *chevalier*, the English called them *cniht*, which was to become, over time, "knight". When a man was dubbed a knight, he was thwacked round the ears – the last blow he would ever receive without retaliating. A Norman knight needed four horses; one to ride to the battle, one (his war-horse – his *destrier*) to ride at the battle, one for his squire and one for his weapons and equipment. It was an expensive business, being a knight.

It was hard work, too. Nobles had small bands of knights, a little like the *huscarls* of the English earls, and these teams – *conrois* – practised tactics and manoeuvres together. They trained hard to become better riders and to become more skilled in the use of the lance or the sword. After all – this was not a game. This was a matter of life or death to these people. They were professionals.

Like most boys of his class, William rode well from an early age. Young trainee knights may have used deliberately heavy practice weapons to develop muscles – strength and stamina were going to be vital in real battles. Boys practised on wheeled wooden horses pulled along by other trainees, aiming their lances at wooden targets.

Sets of *conrois* would ride together – a *conrois* might be as much as 50 men – setting off towards the enemy line in ranks. The saddles had long stirrups so that the knight was almost standing to brace himself. The knights would begin by trotting, to conserve the energy of their precious horses, then spur them to a gallop as they drew nearer to the enemy, riding so close that their knees would almost be touching, holding their lances in front of them and hurtling towards the bloody collision ahead.

Like Harold, William also used mercenaries – hired soldiers from outside the country, whose military training was profitable skill in such warlike times. Mercenaries were often driven by more than mere financial motives, though. They often allied themselves to causes about which they felt strongly and could be heroically loyal to the lord who hired them. Many of the men who fought for William may well have believed themselves to be genuinely on a holy crusade.

It was hard to hold on to troops when so many were mercenaries and adventurers. William tried to stem the tide of desertions by providing for the men at his own expense. In return they were forbidden from plundering the locals. It says a lot about William that he was able to maintain such rigid discipline at Dives. After all there were probably about 10,000 men – soldiers and servants, butchers and cooks, armourers and carpenters – and the camp probably covered more than 90 hectares. So it was no mean feat just to feed everyone.

And then there were the precious war-horses of course. The horses needed hay – tonnes of hay, and straw for bedding. They needed fresh drinking water. They needed to be shod and they needed blacksmiths to make the shoes and nails. And thousands of horses produced lots and lots – and *lots* – of manure! And, of course, the horses were not the only ones. With the waste products of all those men and horses, it is amazing that there seemed to have been no outbreak of disease at Dives.

What is certain is that Dives must have been an unpleasant, noisy, stinking, fly-ridden place that summer. William's men must have been bored and homesick, like all soldiers posted away from their loved ones. They must have been scared, too, like all soldiers before a battle; the older ones remembering the random cruelty of battle, the younger ones dreading the unknown.

But things were about to change – dramatically. Unknown to either William or Harold, one of the other great warriors of the age was about to enter the picture…

Harold
Stamford Bridge
September 1066

HAROLD COULD NOT KEEP the men of the *fyrd* on active duty for ever. These men needed to return to their land. This English army might be massive and intimidating but it would count for nothing if the country starved. That was exactly what would happen if the harvest was not brought in – and that needed men; the very same men who made up the ranks of Harold's great army.

This was the time that people began stocking up their larders for the winter months. The autumn storms would soon begin to blow; no one in their right mind would invade now. Surely they would be safe until the following year.

So, on 8 September 1066 Harold disbanded the *fyrd*, just as William probably knew he would have to do. William knew that however difficult it was for him to keep his men together, Harold of England was having the same problem.

Once again the south coast was undefended. And to

make matters worse Harold knew that if he left his ships along the south coast they would fall foul of the gales that were sure to come. But even as he tried to get them back to the safety of the Thames, many of them were smashed to pieces by one of the very storms from which he had hoped to protect them. How that long-haired star must have haunted Harold. He seemed to be cursed with bad luck – and it was not over yet.

On 19 September, less than a week after his fleet had been mauled by the storm, Harold was in London once more. He had left his manor in Bosham, Sussex, a few days before and had entered the city to a warm welcome. London was pleased to see their king. It made them feel as though things were back to normal; as if the danger had passed.

Disbanding the *fyrd* had been a gamble, but Harold had had no real choice. Even so, he must have had a lot of sleepless nights, not helped by the fact that he was also suffering from terrible, and probably rheumatic, pains in his legs.

Then came the shocking news that an invading army had already landed; not in the south, but in the north. It wasn't the Normans, but a force of Vikings who were already ransacking the coast. They had set fire to the town of Scarborough and butchered its people.

It was time for King Harold to show what he was made of. He had no great army to lead now, but without a moment's hesitation, he gathered his *huscarls* and told them to get their axes and be ready to ride. Despite the pain in his legs, Harold strapped on his sword, threw his suit of mail across his saddle, mounted his horse and, riding at the head of his troops, clattered through the city and off up the old Roman road heading north.

In 1066 Scarborough (now in Yorkshire) was on the coast of Northumbria, which stretched from the Humber northwards all the way to the border with Scotland. Northumbria was under the protection of Earl Morcar and it was up to him to deal with the invaders. He and his brother, Edwin, were the first line of defence. But the teenage earls were out of their depth. This was no ordinary Viking raiding party. This was a massive invasion force, and at its head was Harald Hardrada, King of Norway and one of the most famous fighting men of his day.

Harald Hardrada was a giant blond-haired warrior. He had served on the shores of the Black Sea as commander of the Varangian Guard of the Byzantine Empire. Byzantium, or Constantinople, was a little pocket of the world where Roman civilization lived on after the fall of the Roman Empire. It had street lighting, a sewerage system, aqueducts, libraries, and palaces stuffed full of treasures and wonders from all over the world. As part of the army there, Hardrada had served in Syria and Armenia, Sicily and Bulgaria, getting rich along the way. He may even have travelled to Jerusalem before hauling his loot back to Norway, where he ended up as ruler.

Harald Hardrada's longships had left Bergen in Norway earlier in the month and travelled north to the Norse settlements of the Shetlands and Orkneys, where Harald gathered supporters on the way. From there they sailed south, to Scotland.

The Vikings wreaked havoc along the north-eastern coastline of England and they put ashore at Cleveland. It was said that as Harald jumped ashore he stumbled and fell – a very bad omen. Even so, the Viking warriors outmatched any opposition sent against them.

And there was a new twist. As the Norsemen sailed into the Humber estuary Harald Hardrada now met up once more with the man who had persuaded him to launch this invasion – none other than King Harold's brother, Tostig Godwinson.

Harald had been involved in a vicious fight with his one-time ally, Swein Estrithson, King of Denmark, when Tostig Godwinson turned up to persuade him he really ought to invade England. Tostig had already been to Swein about this, but the Dane was not interested in helping Tostig. At first, Harald Hardrada was not keen either. He said he did not trust Englishmen and neither did he particularly want to face the axes of the fearsome *huscarls*.

Tostig told him that the north would welcome him with open arms; that they were pining for the days of Norse rule. These were lies, or at least half-truths, but Harald allowed himself to be persuaded. Maybe he was greedy. Maybe he was just bored.

Harald Hardrada and Tostig moored their ships on the River Ouse at a place called Ricall. Now the invasion would begin in earnest. The army came ashore and planned their march on York, the Northumbrian capital, about ten miles to the north.

Harald Hardrada's army consisted of men from Orkney and Scotland, as well as Tostig's Englishmen and Flemish mercenaries. He split the force into two parts and took the two roads available, but met no opposition.

Northumbria remained a very different place to the rest of England and there was probably a lot of resentment at being ruled by surly southerners like Edward the Confessor, who could not even be bothered to make the journey north. On top of this, the area had been heavily settled by Scandinavians and there must have been those who were nostalgic for the days of Danelaw; who saw Harald Hardrada as a hero (certainly that's what Tostig had told Harald when he visited him in Norway). Or perhaps, like most civilians in a war-zone, the Northumbrians thought of their families and stayed indoors.

The two roads the Viking army had taken converged again at a place called Gate Fulford and the Norse army regrouped. Up ahead of them they heard the sound of armed men approaching. It was Earl Morcar and his brother, Edwin. It was 20 September and the first great battle of 1066 was about to take place.

Earl Morcar's army was about the same size as that of Hardrada – possibly about 5,000 men – and they blocked the road to York at Gate Fulford. They had a river on one side and a marsh on the other. Maybe Morcar and Edwin thought that this was Tostig's army again. The realization that they were facing the famous Harald Hardrada must have sent a chill down their spines.

Some of the Vikings fought with double-handed axes like the English *huscarls* and though they appear to have been less keen on chain-mail, Harald Hardrada was so taken with his hauberk that he had even given it a name: "Emma". But whatever they fought with, Norsemen had a justifiably fearsome reputation, particularly the legendary Viking *berserkers* – warriors who worked themselves into a kind of furious state of unstoppable blood-lust.

Hardrada had his men form a circular shield wall set up his standard *Landeyder*, meaning "Land Ravager", which was white with a black raven across it, and invited the English to come and get him. The two sides roared their battle cries and the English attacked, smashing into the Viking army's right flank, and cutting a swathe through its ranks.

But Harald Hardrada was an incredibly experienced warrior and he quickly got the better of the opposition. Swords and axes hacked and clashed until the English were forced to flee for their lives.

Unfortunately for them, many fled straight into the bog, where they became sitting ducks as they floundered in the mud in their chain-mail armour. The Norsemen hacked them down and in the end, there were so many

English dead in the mud, it was said that the Vikings could use their bodies as a grisly kind of boardwalk to squelch across the marsh.

If Harold had expected to rely on the northern earls to protect the north while he watched the south, they had let him down. Not only had Morcar and Edwin been defeated, but they had overseen the deaths of hundreds of Englishmen vital to the defence of the country.

On that same day, Harald Hardrada and Tostig Godwinson entered York, which promptly surrendered. Everything seemed to be going well for Hardrada. In one battle he seemed to have brought the whole of the north of England on to his side, just as Tostig had promised. He insisted on hostages from York and the surrounding area to keep his army safe from another attack.

As for the traitorous Tostig, he must have relished his return to his old earldom. Certainly he seemed eager to punish the Northumbrians for their treatment of him. Tostig was happy to collaborate and use his local knowledge to point out the most important hostages to take. The Vikings noisily celebrated their victory. They had shown these puny Englishmen how to fight. For now anyway...

On the evening of 24 September, the Vikings staggered back to Ricall on the River Ouse with all the loot the townsfolk of York had given them to stop them ransacking their city. The people of York had also arranged to get even more supplies in for Harald's troops and the 150 children Harald had demanded as hostages – just in case they changed their minds about being so co-operative. Stamford Bridge on the River Derwent was the chosen spot for the handover that was to take place the following day.

Sure enough, on Monday 25 September, the Vikings squinted bleary-eyed into a bright autumn morning, no doubt nursing hangovers from the celebrations of the night before. It was hot and they had no reason to expect trouble, so they left their helmets, shields and heavy mail armour behind. Swords and bows would be quite enough.

There seemed no need for everyone to go. They were only picking up supplies and taking charge of children. Along with Tostig, Harald took two-thirds of his troops and left the rest back at the ship under the command of Eystein Orri. Everyone was in a good mood and was relaxed. Too relaxed.

Harald and Tostig got the shock of their lives when they saw a huge cloud of dust on the horizon. Slowly, the light began to play across a mass of spear blades, helmets and mail – so many it was said it looked like a *"sheet of ice"*. It was Harold Godwinson at the head of an army.

King Harold and his *huscarls* had ridden day and night from the south of England, covering a staggering 190 miles in five days. Tostig and Harald may have put Edwin and Morcar to flight, but now they were face to face with the mightiest warrior in England.

Harold had arrived in Tadcaster the day before and probably mustered the survivors of Gate Fulford and called men to the *fyrd* in the King's name to build the necessary force. He had rested his men that night and set off for York that morning where he heard the news that his troublesome brother and Harald Hardrada were waiting at Stamford Bridge.

The Norse say that Harold and a force of 20 *huscarls* rode up to the bridge, and Harald, Tostig and group of soldiers went to meet them on the other bank. Harold looked across at his brother and offered him one last chance. He shouted out that if Tostig changed sides, he would get his earldom back. But both men probably knew it was too late.

When Tostig called back and asked what Harald Hardrada would get, Harold replied, *"Six feet of English earth – or much more as he is taller than other men."* Tostig grandly announced that he was not about to betray his ally. As Harold turned and rode back to his troops he must have thought how easily Tostig was prepared to betray his own family and his own country.

But Harald Hardrada's English was poor, and he had no idea that the man on the other bank had been Harold Godwinson. When Tostig told him, Harald said that if he had known his identity he would have killed him there and then. This was fighting talk. But now the time for talk was over.

Harold's men went straight for the bridge, but a small contingent of Vikings bravely fought them off, buying time for Hardrada to organize his troops on the other side of the river. Hardrada sent a messenger back to Ricall and formed a circular shield wall, once more planting his *Landeyder* standard.

At one point the bridge was held by a lone Norse warrior – a giant wielding a battle-axe and felling Harold's men like saplings. The English were so impressed they offered him mercy if he laid down his arms, but he merely called them cowards and waved them on. Finally, the English sent a boat underneath the bridge with a man with a spear on board. When he was in just the right place, he rammed his spear up between the planking of the bridge and into the unfortunate Viking.

At three o'clock in the afternoon, Harold's men had hacked their way across the bridge and were face to face with the enemy. Hardrada's army was outnumbered and horribly under-equipped, but they were still Vikings. They flew at the English and the two armies crashed headlong into each other, yelling, jabbing, cutting and hacking. The air was filled with the rasp of metal against metal, the shouts of the warriors, the screams of the wounded. The Vikings fought bravely, but it was a lost cause. They were hacked and beaten down, until even the shield wall was slashed open.

On seeing this, Harald Hardrada himself burst out of his protective ring like a *berserker* and thundered towards the English wearing a bright blue tunic over his mail hauberk and wielding a sword two-handed. An arrow hit him in the windpipe and he fell to the ground. It was a warrior's death for the last great Viking raider.

Harold had no great desire to lose any more men, with William still to deal with, so he offered the Vikings the chance to surrender. Harald Hardrada was dead, so why carry on? The Norsemen could go back to Norway and that would be that. Go home! Live!

But Tostig Godwinson had different ideas. Looking across at his brother, he walked over and stood beside Harald Hardrada's *Landeyder* standard and made it clear that he was for fighting on. This was personal.

The remaining warriors stood firm. The Vikings bellowed out their defiance. If this was the last stand of the Vikings then it would be a fitting end, a bloody end. No surrender. To the death!

Harold did not want a fight, but if there was going to be a fight, so be it. The English hurled themselves at the invaders. The English took heavy casualties, but the outcome was never in doubt. Tostig Godwinson was killed along with many of his Flemish mercenaries, and soon the bulk of the Viking force was dead or dying.

But no sooner had Harold gained victory over this part of the Viking force, than Eystein Orri arrived at the head of the rest. When Hardrada's messengers had arrived at Ricall, Eystein and the others had hurriedly put on their armour, picked up their axes and swords and set off to Stamford Bridge. Now Eystein picked up the *Landeyder* standard and urged the Vikings on again.

Sweltering in their heavy mail and helmets and worn

out from the march, the Vikings still managed to charge headlong into the startled English, who gathered their senses, held their line and slugged it out, toe to toe, teeth to teeth, sword to bloody sword.

Again it was the Vikings who came off second-best. Eystein fell and so did most of the Viking command, and as night drew in, those who were able used the darkness to escape back to their longships. The English had lost far too many men, but the Vikings had been utterly decimated. Most of the dead were never buried and when the crows had finished, there was still a *"mountain of bones"* to mark the spot for years after.

One of the few Viking commanders who actually managed to escape from the battle was Hardrada's marshal, Styrkar. He was making his getaway in only his shirt when he came across a man driving a horse and cart. He asked to buy the man's leather coat, but the man gave him a hard time for being on the losing side. Styrkar cut off his head, took the coat *and* the horse, and set off by road to Ricall.

The Viking leadership had now fallen to Hardrada's son, Olaf Haraldson. He could see no point in fighting on, and King Harold had no desire to lose even more men. The Vikings were allowed to go in peace and Olaf (who, in stark contrast to his father, became known as Olaf the Quiet) went home to Norway to rule with his brother, Magnus.

As the longships sailed out into the North Sea, the victorious Englishmen could relax and count their blessings. Swords and axes were salvaged from the battlefield and armour stripped from the dead.

Just as after every battle in history, those who had so recently cheated death felt the sweetness of life more keenly than before. Brothers sought out brothers, friends clapped each other on the back, sharing in each other's good fortune, grateful that the blood that stained their tunics was the blood of others. Tales would be told and retold, the Viking opponents growing taller and wilder at each new telling.

And just as after any battle in history, the laughter of the lucky ones mingled with the groans and screams of the injured and the calls of those for whom there would be no happy reunion; brother calling vainly for brother, and men searching through the dead and dying for the face of a friend they half-hoped they would not find.

It must have been a bittersweet victory for Harold. The Godwinson clan was often its own worst enemy. Harold's brother Svein had murdered his own cousin and now his brother Tostig lay dead among a foreign force he had helped to lead.

Harold must have known, too, that he had been fortunate at Stamford Bridge. His men had faced the Viking army in two disadvantaged stages – one part under-equipped, the other exhausted by a forced march. But even so, Harold had made his own luck by his bold tactics. This was a great English victory, by any reckoning, and Harold could take the credit for it.

If the Battle of Stamford Bridge had been the only

battle Harold had fought in 1066 he would probably have gone down in history as one of the greatest warrior kings of England. He must have felt as though he had beaten his run of bad luck and that his reign had not been doomed by the long-haired star after all.

But the Vikings were not the only threat to England in 1066 and this would not be the only battle. William of Normandy was still across the Channel, waiting to pounce – and now Harold was way up in the north.

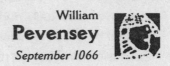
AFTER WEEKS OF NOTHING but winds blowing from the north, finally the direction changed and the fleet could sail. The horses had eaten every blade of grass around Dives and William was not going to be able to hold his men together for ever with promises of riches and glory. If there was going to be an invasion, it had to come soon.

William ordered his fleet to load up and set sail on 12 September, but the same gales that had wrecked Harold's ships now wreaked havoc with William's. Several of his ships sank in open sea and others were wrecked on Ponthieu's treacherous coast – the very same coast that Harold Godwinson had been washed up on two years before.

There is some confusion about whether William was heading for England at this point or moving his men to another harbour, but whichever it was, it was certainly a disaster. Many men were drowned before the surviving ships sailed into the town of Saint-Valéry-sur-Somme, 160 miles up the coast. There were even rumours that William had many more men buried secretly so as not to damage morale. It did not bode well for the trip across the Channel. It had shown what most men had known already, that these ships were at the mercy of the winds and once aboard they would be, too.

It was autumn now. Rain poured down and the winds had once again turned south and blew mockingly into William's face. Even the arrival of the papal banner from Rome would not have done much to raise the men's spirits. They must have wondered whether God was on their side after all. Men began to slip away quietly and head home. William's invasion plan was starting to fall apart.

The holy crusade against the English needed a miracle. William ordered the body of Saint Valéry himself to be taken from his tomb in the town's church and brought outside to work some divine magic on his disgruntled troops. William and his men made offerings to the saint's relics. Maybe some of the men prayed that William might call the whole thing off and let them all go home before even more of them ended up at the bottom of the Channel, but there was no doubt what William prayed for.

William was said to have had his eyes constantly fixed on the weather vane of the church of Saint-Valéry, waiting for the wind to change. Finally, on the evening of

27 September, two days after Harold's victorious battle with the Vikings at Stamford Bridge, William's prayers were answered. It was the miracle he needed. Saint Valéry had worked his magic on the wind. The crusade was back on.

The ships were loaded with everything from chain-mail to barrels of wine. They had to move fast if they were going to make the afternoon tide. Then the men and horses came aboard. Many men must have feared the voyage more than the idea of battle; and rightly so. There was real danger, just in getting the men, arms and particularly horses across miles of open water. If the horses panicked out at sea it would be a chaos of flailing hooves and all that shifting weight could overturn the ships.

They were to leave at night, moving downstream following William's flagship, the *Mora*, which would wait offshore. They were to follow his lantern. With luck they would be in England in 12 hours' time.

The Bayeux Tapestry shows the *Mora* with the leopard of Normandy on its prow and a row of shields along the sides in the old Viking tradition. William ordered each ship to carry lanterns and torches and, to help keep the fleet in formation, they were to use trumpet calls to stay in contact with one another.

William would have had the best helmsmen and pilots aboard his ship, men who knew the crossing and knew the English coast, and he would need them. They had no compass or indeed any kind of navigation system other than experience and an occasional glimpse of the Pole Star when the clouds broke for a minute or two. Many prayers must have been said that night as the Normans huddled together in the moonless dark of the open sea.

And when the dawn brought welcome light, it also brought an unwelcome shock for the men of the *Mora*. They were on their own! The sail was dropped and the *Mora* came to a bobbing halt.

William ordered someone to climb the mast to try to spot the rest of the fleet. There was nothing in sight. Staring into the wide empty horizon, the crew began to get restless; the fears they already had were about to tip over into panic, but William calmly ordered breakfast, poured himself a glass of wine and told everyone to wait.

Whatever feelings William had, he was going to show his men nothing but confidence. When he sent someone up the mast half an hour later, four Norman ships were spotted on the horizon. A little later, the whole invasion fleet was sighted.

If Harold had been a little lucky at Stamford Bridge, then William had been *incredibly* lucky on his Channel crossing. If he had hit gales in open sea, as the Spanish Armada was to do four centuries later, it would have been a very different story. And since Harold had been forced to disband the fleet, William had not had to face the far more experienced English sailors in open waters.

The Normans arrived off the south coast on the morning of 28 September. The white cliffs at Beachy Head standing out on the horizon must have been a welcome first sign of England for the nervous Norman troops. They were nearing Pevensey in Sussex. It was probably about ten o'clock.

Today, this part of the coast is littered with reminders that this is England's weak spot, its exposed underbelly where the crossing from Europe is shortest – from Martello Towers built at the beginning of the nineteenth century to guard against Napoleon, to the Second World War air-bases guarding against the threat of German invasion in the 1940s.

There were plenty of Normans moving around the country under Edward the Confessor so William must have been able to get fairly detailed information about the layout of the south coast of England. He may not have aimed specifically for Pevensey in advance, but once he was there, he probably knew what to expect.

The coastline from Hastings to Pevensey is one long shingle bank now, but in 1066 there was a series of inlets and busy harbours. There was also a tidal lagoon at Pevensey, long since silted up, with a shingle bank between it and the sea, passable at high tide, and mud-flats all around. On the western side of the lagoon there was a peninsula with the ruins of a stone-built Roman fort.

William's pilots would probably have told him that to get the ships into the harbour they would have to wait for the surge of water that came with the incoming tide to lift them over the shingle bank at its mouth – otherwise they would have to leave the ships exposed.

So William waited for the tide to change and, at about eleven o'clock, the Normans put ashore, archers jumping down first to provide cover, soldiers next, scrunching their boats into the shingle. The second invasion of 1066 had begun.

Just as Harald Hardrada is supposed to have done, legend has it that William stumbled as he set foot ashore. William would have been perfectly aware that this was considered a bad omen, so he lifted up handfuls of shingle and shouted that he was seizing his new kingdom in both hands. And what is more, it looked as though he was going to do so without any resistance. There wasn't an English soldier in sight.

That doesn't mean, of course, that the place was deserted or that no one saw William coming. The sails of his approaching ships would have been visible for a long time before they landed. The *fyrd* may have been disbanded, but the local *thegns* still had a responsibility to their earl and to their king. The warning would have been sent straight away, by rider or beacon.

Harold had had troops in Pevensey all summer. He had realized that this might be a possible landing site for a Norman invasion and stationed a lot of men there. But now the men of the *fyrd* were back in their villages and blissfully unaware of what was going on. Harold had left men at Romney and Dover, but left Pevensey and Hastings undefended. This was a big mistake.

William ordered the rest of his men to start disembarking and they began bringing the horses and supplies ashore. If Harold's men had still been here, the Duke's men would probably have suffered huge losses on that unprotected shingle beach, with the sea at their backs, but instead they could calmly unload their boats unopposed.

Just in case Harold's men suddenly turned up, William got his men to work on the old Roman fort. Ironically Pevensey Castle had been built by the Romans to guard against attacks by Harold's Anglo-Saxon ancestors and was the largest of the Forts of the Saxon Shore, as they were called. Pevensey Castle was huge, even after being abandoned for four centuries, covering an area of about three and a half hectares, with walls up to seven-and-a-half-metres high and three-metres thick.

Inside these massive walls – which still stand today – the Normans built a wooden fort. William may have even brought it with him across the Channel in kit form. The Norman skill in castle-building was going to be crucial to William's invasion plans, allowing him to defend the towns he conquered. William then sent a scouting party of archers to check out the area and report back.

The scouts told him that the way was clear and William sent knights to the town of Hastings, demanding its surrender. A party of Norman knights must have come as a very unpleasant surprise to the people of Hastings, but without Harold's men to defend them, they had no real choice. William took his first English town without even breaking out into a sweat.

William then moved his fleet to Hastings and had his men build a fort on top of the cliffs. They set to work with picks and shovels and made a steep hill, called a motte, and topped it with a wooden keep. It must have been a chilling sight for the English. This was no raid; the Normans were obviously planning to stay.

The English also got their first taste of Norman ruthlessness. The villages and harbours between Pevensey and Hastings were attacked, looted and burned, and William's men plundered the local countryside. The Normans stole food, and slaughtered livestock and hauled it back to the beach where it was cooked and eaten.

William's men did not just steal. They also destroyed. This was a classic Norman tactic, one that they had already used to devastating effect in Europe. Houses and outbuildings were burned to the ground as the terrified inhabitants stood by, powerless to do anything about it.

It is doubtful whether William could have stopped this destruction happening even if he had wanted to – it is amazing that he had kept such a grip on his men and stopped it happening in Normandy – but it suited William to make the local English suffer. They were under Harold's protection both as Earl and as King. William wanted to force Harold to come to their aid.

Harold

The Hoar Apple Tree

October 1066

HAROLD WAS NOW in completely the wrong place. He knew he had no choice but to return south to counter the threat from William. His army was not fit for another fight, so he decided to ride for London taking only his *huscarls* with him. Before he left York, though, he made two serious mistakes.

Firstly, he made the decision not to divide the plunder from Stamford Bridge among his men. Instead he put it in the safekeeping of Ealdred, Archbishop of York. It is not clear *why* he did this. He may simply have wanted the loot for himself to cover the expenses of wars to come, but whatever the reason, the army was outraged. There were many desertions and few volunteers for his call to march south against the Norman invaders.

Harold's second mistake was in his dealings with those slippery northern earls of his, Morcar and Edwin. He made it clear that he did not really trust them by appointing a deputy to rule in the north while he was away. Morcar and Edwin were not amused. Harold may not have trusted them, but he should not have made it so obvious. The brothers took offence – but then they probably had no intention of helping Harold anyway. They would have been very pleased to hear that Tostig was dead, but not to hear that Harold had offered him their earldoms before he was killed. No, they were going to stand back and see who won before picking sides. They may even have come to the conclusion that a Norman victory would be a good thing. England was a big country. William might be persuaded to leave the north to their rule in return for their submission to his authority. It was the revival of the old dream of an independent Northumbria. They clearly did not know William at all.

Harold and his *huscarls* galloped south and somewhere on route he heard the awful news that William had already landed and the Normans were torching the villages of Sussex. Harold had just achieved a great victory over the Vikings, but he knew that this was the big one. The Normans were going to be a much more difficult enemy to beat.

They pushed on with even greater urgency and arrived in London on 5 October. But instead of riding directly back to London, Harold had taken a detour and travelled to Waltham, to the abbey he had built and endowed with money when Edward was still king. He spent the day in prayer and then left for London, where, it is said, he received a message from Duke William.

The messenger was a monk called Hugh Margot. Hugh brought an offer from William that they could put their rival claims to the English throne to an independent judge. William may have even offered to meet Harold in single combat.

How serious this suggestion was – if it was ever made – with William already ashore and terrorizing the south coast, it is difficult to say. But the offer and Hugh's repetition of the Norman claim to the English crown only succeeded in enraging Harold. This may, of course, have been what William wanted; to rile Harold into making a rash decision instead of weighing up all the alternatives.

Harold was probably also told that William carried the papal banner and ring. Harold had to face the truth that with no opportunity to put his side of the argument about the alleged oath, the Pope had come down in favour of William. God – or at least his representative on Earth – seemed to have deserted England, just as Edward had prophesied.

Instead of negotiating a peace settlement with William, Harold is said to have sent Hugh Margot packing. God would decide who was the rightful king. He started planning his assault on the Norman forces. Harold seemed determined to march on Hastings and get to grips with William straight away, before reinforcements could be sent from Normandy. But his brother, Gyrth, urged caution.

Gyrth Godwinson pointed out that Harold was physically exhausted from the last few days' exertions, and that they needed time to gather more troops. They could not expect to take on the Normans with the available men. Why not buy some time? In any case, would it not be better that he, Gyrth, lead the troops against William? Then if he was beaten, England would still have a king and Harold would still be able to mount a second attack on the invaders. Meanwhile why not give the Normans a taste of their own medicine and burn everything between Hastings and London? William and his men would be forced to march through a desert without supplies and in the meantime, the English could regroup.

It was a brutally simple idea that might well have worked, but Harold would not listen. If he had, things might have turned out very differently. But Harold was no Ethelred the Unready or Edward the Confessor. He was a warrior king, and warrior kings lead their men into battle. Besides, Harold was probably giddy with confidence after Stamford Bridge.

Harold felt that he could not stand by idly while the Normans attacked his people in Sussex. He was duty bound, as William knew he was, to protect them. That was how it worked. That was how a lord gained loyalty; that was how a king gained loyalty. If Harold did not fight for *them*, how could he expect them to fight for *him*?

Harold's idea was to strike immediately; to march on Hastings and engage the Normans in a decisive battle. It had worked against Hardrada, so why not William? He would force the Normans into the peninsula at Hastings, trap them there without food and then cut off any escape by sea with his navy. It could work.

And so, only a few days after arriving in London, Harold was at the head of an army heading south once more. With him were his brothers, Gyrth and Leofwine, and Hakon, the nephew he had brought back from Normandy. Harold's partner, Edith Swan-neck, may even have been at the rear of the army as they headed south.

The force was made up of Harold's own elite force of *huscarls*, *thegns* from London, and men called up by the *fyrd* from the south and East Anglia. Harold also had mercenaries – some of whom may have been sent by Swein Estrithson, the King of Denmark, a nephew of Harold's mother. It was Swein Estrithson's brother, Bjorn, whom Svein Godwinson had murdered, but he does not seem to have borne Harold a grudge. Estrithson also had good reason to be grateful to see the back of his old enemy, Harald Hardrada.

After marching nearly 60 miles over three days, Harold and his men emerged from the great forest of the Andredsweald out on to the South Downs late at night on 13 October. Friday the 13th – not the most auspicious date to arrive at a battlefield.

Harold led his men out of the forest to the muster point on Caldbeck Hill; a hill just south of the forest, at the intersection of two tracks marked by an ancient apple tree. This Hoar Apple Tree was where Harold would assemble his troops and prepare for battle.

Whether he intended a surprise attack similar to the one he had used with Harald Hardrada's men or simply intended to box in the Normans until their supplies ran out, is not clear. He may even have planned a night attack. Either way, William had his own ideas.

William
Telham Hill
October 1066

SOME TIME AROUND Harold's visit to Waltham, Duke William had received a message from one of the Normans living in England – Robert fitzWymark, the man who had been with Harold at King Edward's deathbed.

Robert was related to William on his mother's side, but he seemed to have ignored this. Instead of an encouraging message welcoming William and wishing him well, Robert's words were very harsh indeed. He said that King Harold had just gained an incredible victory over the Norsemen. He said that Harold was heading William's way with a massive army and that William's army was no match for it. He warned William to stay inside his defences or he was going to be crushed.

But William knew that Harold's forces would be depleted, and that Harold and his *huscarls* must be exhausted. Let Harold and his men come. The last thing William wanted was for Harold to delay and gather more troops.

William may also have received word from Hugh Margot, the messenger monk who would have ridden from London with Harold's reply. If there had been any doubt in William's mind that he would have to fight for the English crown, Harold's reply made things crystal clear.

When Norman scouts saw English spears glinting in the darkness of the woods they raced back to tell William in Hastings. William put the whole camp on high alert all through the night in case the English tried a surprise night-attack. The Normans started to think of what lay ahead and priests were busy hearing confessions all through the hours of darkness.

Then William spoke to his men. He told them that they would need courage in the fight ahead, that retreat was impossible, that defeat would mean certain death. He gave a gruesome account of the butchery of Stamford Bridge.

Even Harold's victory against Hardrada was put to work in William's favour. He may have persuaded his troops to see the Vikings as their kinsmen. The Normans had once been Vikings, after all. And had not Harold killed his own brother? The Normans even put it about that Harold had mutilated Tostig's corpse, having its head lopped off. That was what they were up against. A murderer. A man who had broken his oath.

They, on the other hand, had God on their side. This was a crusade blessed by the Pope. If he, William, were victorious, he would build an abbey on the site of the battle, with the altar on the very place where Harold's standard now fluttered. William called for a mass to be held and attended it himself. Round his neck he placed the relics upon which Harold had supposedly sworn his oath two years before.

Dawn broke a little after five o'clock. It was Saturday 14 October. The Normans set off following the papal banner along the old Roman road towards the great expanse of the Andredsweald. First came the archers, then the infantry, then the cavalry, with William himself leading his best knights. Seven miles later they came to the top of Telham Hill at Hecheland (now called Blackhorse Hill), and saw the English army ahead, blocking the route to London. William gathered his men in readiness for the advance.

William rode in the centre with his Norman elite, a standard-bearer and a party of archers. On William's left were men from Brittany, Maine and Anjou; on the right, French and Flemish troops under William fitzOsbern and Eustace of Boulogne – the same Eustace whose men had caused a riot in Dover and triggered the quarrel between King Edward and the Godwins.

When William and his men reached the bottom of Telham Hill, he and the other Norman knights put on their chain-mail armour and William mounted his horse – a gift from the King of Spain. William carried a mace –

but it may also have been a kind of baton – a symbol of his authority.

It is said that in an uncharacteristic show of nerves, he managed to put his hauberk on back to front. Knowing how superstitious his soldiers were, he laughed off this potential bad omen by saying, *"Thus shall my dukedom be turned into a kingdom."*

Harold
The Fighting Man
14 October 1066

THE ENGLISH WERE strung out for half a mile along a ridge, crossing and blocking the way to London, facing south towards the Normans. Harold was in the centre at the highest point of the ridge with his standards. One was the red windsock-style Dragon of Wessex, which stirred memories of Alfred the Great's victory over the Danes; the other was Harold's own personal battle standard – the Fighting Man. This probably had an image of a warrior on it, decorated with gold threads and precious stones.

The best armed and armoured men stood to the front of the line; experienced warriors such as the *huscarls* and Harold's brothers, Gyrth and Leofwine. Behind them were the men called up to the *fyrd*, from Sussex and Kent. These men probably stood in ranks, with Harold on slightly higher ground to view the scene. There would have been a bodyguard of men around Harold to protect him.

The previous night, by the light of campfires, nervous farmers who had never seen a battle in their lives had listened, spellbound, to the heroes of Stamford Bridge, trying to soak up some of their courage. They would need it. The professional warriors would have been well-armed and well-armoured, but some of the lower ranks were armed with nothing more than slingshots and clubs, with no armour at all.

But Harold's army was in a reasonably good position. They held the high ground and the ridge sloped sharply to the south and to the east. Although Harold did not have cavalry and does not seem to have had archers, he did have the fearsome *huscarls*, and they formed a shield wall at the front and flanks of the army.

The shrubs and woodland round them made it very difficult for William to go around the English army and outmanoeuvre them. The Normans would have to come at them head on. On the other hand, if things went wrong, it was going to be very difficult to get away once the battle began. In front of the ridge, the land fell away towards an area of marshy ground, crossed by the Hastings road. The slope in front of them was called *Santlache*, meaning Sandy Stream. It would later be called *Senlac,* or Blood Lake, by the Normans.

But the English had been caught on the hop – they were certainly not expecting William to make an appearance so soon, and their men were not all in place;

troops were still coming out of the forest and taking their positions. If Gyrth was not actually saying, "I told you so," to his brother, he must have thought it. If only Harold had waited for more men. Harold had hoped to surprise the Normans, but William had probably got the jump on them instead.

Added to that it was a bit of a squeeze up there on that narrow ridge. The English were hemmed into a small space, and would have to be disciplined if the shield wall was not going to be breached by the Norman cavalry. It was said that many men left at this point because they were not happy with the cramped conditions. And it is easy to see how men might lose their nerve as they stood shoulder to shoulder waiting for the Normans to charge. Some may even have felt they were simply not needed, there were so many men there already.

But surely Harold only had to hold out until the next day, when reinforcements would arrive. Time was against William, not Harold. They were sure to win, he told his men, as long as they held firm. Who were these Normans anyway? What match were they for English axes?

William
The Shield Wall
14 October 1066

WILLIAM'S MEN PROBABLY moved along the trackway in columns before spreading out on either side of it to take up positions opposite the English lines. At about eight o'clock, the mainly Breton contingent wheeled left to take the western side, while Eustace of Boulogne and the men from France, Picardy and Flanders wheeled right.

William took centre stage with the papal banner. He led the Norman contingent, surrounded by his kinsmen and most trusted knights. William's half-brother, Odo, was there. He was Bishop Odo of Bayeux now.

In front of each cavalry section were the infantry; in front of them, the archers and crossbowmen. Above them on the ridge was the intimidating barrier of the English shield wall. It was clear that conditions were hardly ideal for William's cavalry. He was going to have little alternative than to take the bulk of his force straight up a slippery grass slope, crossing the ground at the bottom, which was waterlogged.

It is impossible to be sure how many men were there that day on either side, but there were certainly thousands. Harold probably had more men than William, despite the fact that Morcar and Edwin had failed to appear with their share of troops. It must have been an incredible sight.

Legend has it that William called for a Norman volunteer to challenge one of the English to single combat. A grand display of heroics was what was called for. They would show the English what they were made of. Supposedly, a minstrel called Taillefer rode forward, juggling his sword and singing the *Song of Roland*, an epic poem about a famous French hero. Taillefer dashed forward, managing to kill one of the English with his lance and another with his sword, before being set upon and hacked down by the English line.

Now the battle could start for real. It was about nine o'clock in the morning. Trumpets were sounded by both sides. William's first move was to send in archers and crossbowmen. These archers were there merely to terrorize the enemy lines, by firing a volley of arrows and crossbow bolts straight at face height, but they had little real effect as they were firing uphill and the arrows thudded into the shield wall or whistled over English heads.

William's infantry marched forward singing the *Song of*

Roland in Taillefer's honour. The English banged their shields and yelled their war cries – *"Oli-Crosse!"* (Holy Cross) and *"Godemite!"* (God Almighty). When the Normans came within range of the English, they were pelted with javelins, hatchets, stones from slingshots and wooden clubs.

And when the Normans finally made it to the shield wall things got even worse. Despite loud calls of *"Dex Aie!"* (God our aid) the Normans were hacked, stabbed, slashed and run through with sickening ease.

The English sang the kind of shanty sailors sing to the rhythm of their work; a kind of football-terrace chant. And with the sound of axes and swords providing the percussion, William's men were impaled and tossed back down the hill to the sound of *"Ut! Ut!"* (Out! Out!).

The Norman infantry kept on and on until no one had the nerve to continue. Having seen what had happened to his foot soldiers, William made the surprising decision to repeat the exercise with his cavalry.

The Norman cavalry were heavily armed and armoured. The war-horses had to charge uphill, carrying all that weight on their backs, and the horses had no protection at all. When they got to the shield wall the *huscarls* were there to greet them, wielding their huge, double-handed axes, cutting through rider and horse alike, lopping off limbs, smashing through shields and crunching through chain-mail.

The Bretons on William's left flank were being hacked to pieces. Their nerve broke, and they turned and galloped back down the hill. Normans, too, began to retreat under the onslaught and were panicked by the rumour that William himself had fallen in the attack.

Breton horsemen were floundering in the boggy ground at the bottom of the hill, and now inexperienced English *fyrdsmen* had a sudden rush of blood to the head and decided to chase after the Bretons. The *fyrdsmen* thought it was all over. But it wasn't.

William *had* been thrown from his horse during the attack, but he was far from finished. The Duke got to his feet and mounted a new horse. He blocked the path of his retreating men. He took off his helmet to show his face to his wavering men. Bishop Odo frantically pointed William out to his men. "*Look at me*," bellowed William. "*I'm still alive. With God's help I shall win.*" He told them that victory was in front of them. Behind them was certain death.

The noise of the battle was deafening, so just in case anyone had not heard what he was saying, William grabbed a spear and began whacking at any retreating Bretons within reach. Some of the other Norman commanders did the same, until the men finally stood their ground.

Fortunes changed swiftly. The Normans rallied around the remounted William and he led an assault on the misguided English *fyrdsmen* who had run down the hill. These isolated Englishmen didn't stand a chance against the Norman war-horses. The English needed to move together or not at all. It may be that Harold actually

Harold is crowned King of England by Archbishop Stigand on
6 January 1066 on the day of King Edward the Confessor's funeral.
(Details from the Bayeux Tapestry reproduced by special permission
of the City of Bayeux.)

The "Long-haired Star" (Halley's Comet) appears over Harold's court
at Westminster, and the new King is told of the bad omen.

William's men load coats of mail, swords, helmets, spears and barrels of wine on their ships as they prepare to invade. The heavy chain-mail hauberks are being carried on poles between two men.

William's army cross the Channel packed with their horses into the newly built ships.

Once safely ashore in England, William sets his men to work building a castle at Hastings.

William is kept informed of Harold's position. Meanwhile his men start burning nearby villages and terrorizing the local people.

William's knights charge the English shield wall. The bottom of the tapestry changes from decorative pictures of animals to a border of dead and mutilated bodies on the battle field.

The Normans and their horses flounder at the bottom of the ridge held by Harold's army.

William lifts his helmet to show his army that he is still alive.
Eustace of Boulogne, holding the papal banner, points him out to the men.

Harold's brothers, Leofwine (left with battle-axe) and Gyrth
(standing with spear), are both killed by Norman knights.

The death of Harold: the tapestry shows the famous image of Harold hit in the eye with an arrow, but the figure on the right is possibly also Harold being struck down by a Norman knight wielding a sword.

ordered an attack and sent part of his army down the hill, but if he did, it had gone badly wrong. It was at about this time that Harold's brothers, Gyrth and Leofwine, were killed in the chaos of the battle.

One unlikely, but not impossible, account has William himself killing Gyrth Godwinson. Gyrth threw a spear at William, but only hit his horse. The Duke then drew his sword, rushed at Gyrth and hacked him to pieces. Whatever the truth, Gyrth's death was a tragedy for Harold and for England.

This was the disaster that Gyrth himself had forseen. Either Gyrth should have gone on his own to meet William, or should have stayed in London while Harold led the army. Now the three Godwinson brothers had been placed in danger, with no one in reserve to mount a counterattack if the Normans won at Hastings. Two of the brothers now lay dead. Everything depended on Harold.

Once again, William seems to have been knocked from his horse. It is said that he called to a knight from Maine to give up his horse but the knight refused. William was outraged. In a fury, he knocked the knight off his horse, and mounted it himself. But the knight was not going to be treated like that by anybody, and promptly struck William, knocking him off again and sending him sprawling, half-dazed, to the ground. At this, William's bodyguard stepped in and killed the disloyal knight.

Then there was a pause in the action. The battle had gone on for hours. Both sides had suffered heavy losses and neither had made any real headway. Harold knew that he had to hold out until nightfall and wait for reinforcements.

Warriors on both sides rested, thanked their stars that they were still alive and prayed they still would be at the end of the day. Below the English shield wall, the Normans watered their horses.

Wounds were tended to as best they could be. Deep cuts might have been stitched or cauterized (burned with hot irons to seal the wound) and all without anaesthetic, of course. Apart from herbal poultices there would have been no real treatment either. Wounds often became contaminated and septic. In 1066 you could die of a small flesh wound or a broken bone.

Blacksmiths and armourers went to work doing running repairs on chain-mail, reweaving the metal links to close tears. Dents in helmets could be beaten out and swords straightened for the next clash. Priests moved through the men, offering prayers and administering the last rights. The dead were dragged away and stripped of armour and weapons.

But then the battle started up once more. William had his men set to work on those inexperienced *fyrdsmen* on the English right flank; men who stood between the Normans and the shield wall ... and Harold himself. William sent in the Breton cavalry again with orders to flee as they had done before. This time the flight was pretence, of course, but the English did not know that. Harold watched in frustration as the *fyrdsmen* did exactly what they had done the last time; they ran hell for leather after the Bretons down the hill.

But, of course, as soon as they got to the bottom of the hill, the Bretons again wheeled their horses round and charged straight at them, lopping them down. The English ran for their lives but were once again easily overtaken and struck down.

There is some argument about this "feigned retreat" of William's. Some people say that eleventh-century battles were too chaotic for this kind of manoeuvre to be pulled off successfully, but William had used it before. In 1053, when King Henry of France had invaded Normandy, William had defeated Henry's ally, Enguerrand of Ponthieu, at St-Aubin-sur-Scies by using exactly the same ploy. Some of the Normans pretended to run away and lured the enemy to break ranks and follow. The Normans then turned about and cut them down.

But at Hastings, the bulk of Harold's men had not moved. William still had not managed to dislodge the English from the top of the ridge and the scene on the slope was one of utter carnage, littered with the dead of both sides; strewn with the corpses of men and horses, body parts, armour and broken weapons.

Exhausted Norman war-horses scrabbled on the churned-up earth, slippery with blood. Their riders spurred them on, but their hooves skidded on shields and coats of mail; snorting through their nostrils with the effort and the pain of exertion. Mud-spattered knights, whose horses had been killed under them, staggered up the hill on foot, sword in hand, teeth clenched to throw themselves once more at the English wall.

The Dragon of Wessex

14 October 1066

THE BATTLE HAD BEEN a close-run thing so far, but Harold and his men were on home soil. They had held the high ground, making each enemy charge exhausting for horses and infantrymen alike. The shield wall had been a match for the Norman attacks and at least Harold had the possibility of reinforcements.

But the English had suffered huge losses — those ill-judged pursuits had taken their toll. The wall was beginning to thin. Harold knew that if William was ever going to break the wall, he had to do it then and a volley of Norman arrows rained down on the English lines.

Harold and his men braced themselves as William mustered his knights and charged full pelt at their lines. Harold's *huscarls* fought back with appalling ferocity, whirling their axes at the oncoming cavalry, but William succeeded in breaking through.

Now it was all or nothing. The fighting became bloodier, and more and more brutal. It was now as much a test of physical strength and stamina as it was skill. It became an effort for the men just to stand up under the weight of their chain-mail.

It was said that one of William's commanders, Robert fitzErnais, made a bid for glory, fought his way up the hill and made straight for the English standard, hacking a path forward with his sword before being felled by Harold's axemen.

Amazingly, it appears that William managed to get thrown to the ground yet again. He was right in the midst of the crazed fighting when it happened and found himself coming off worst in single combat, before being rescued by his men. William had a charmed life it seemed. He was as lucky as Harold was unlucky.

But then luck was essential in a fight like this. Javelins and lances jabbed from every direction, and axes and swords thrust and hacked away. Meanwhile it was increasingly difficult to keep a footing on ground that was slippery with the blood of the fallen. Bodies were strewn everywhere; the roars of the living fought to be heard above the choking cries of the dying, and the squeals of injured horses. The air was filled with the hammering and clanging of a blacksmith's yard and the stench of a slaughterhouse.

And it is was at this point that England suffered the worst blow of all; Harold himself was struck down. There is a well-known tradition that Harold was hit in the eye by an arrow, but this is by no means certain. The Bayeux Tapestry does show a figure next to the word "Harold" being hit in the eye by an arrow, but is it Harold or one of his bodyguards?

There are various versions of his death, including a very unlikely attack by William and a hand-picked group of knights, who charged at Harold; one stabbing him in the chest, one disembowelling him, another lopping off his head and the rest chopping off his leg. And the "leg" reference might be a touch of coyness on behalf of the translators. Some say they castrated him.

Next to the figure with the arrow in the eye on the Bayeux Tapestry is another being struck down by a Norman knight. There is a theory that *both* figures are Harold; the first showing him hit by an arrow, the second showing him being finished off by the knight. There even seems to have been an arrow in the second figure's face, but the stitching has come away.

The fact is, we simply do not know how Harold died; it may be that no one actually saw him fall in all the confusion of battle. But an arrow in the face, however grisly it seems, was certainly not an unusual injury in an eleventh-century battle; Tostig and Harald Hardrada were both said to have been killed by arrows – Hardrada by a shot to the windpipe.

Harold could very well have been hit in the eye and, if not killed outright, certainly would have been in no condition to defend himself from attack by a knight. Although it has been argued over for a long time, *how*

Harold died is less important than what happened next. With the English King dead, the result of the battle was, from this point, never really in doubt. But it was not over yet.

Harold's *huscarls* knew that they were finished and as the sun went down they fought like cornered wolves. They would never surrender and the Normans knew it. Now was their chance to be heroes and die a glorious death; a death that might be sung about in years to come. Just like in the poem, *The Battle of Maldon*, *"The irons would take them, point or edge."*

Their duty was to die with their lord and they went at the Normans until the last of them was finally brought down to lie with his fallen comrades on the blood-soaked English battle line. Harold's Fighting Man and Dragon standards were finally taken.

Unlike the ferocious *huscarls*, the *fyrdsmen* were less inclined to give up their lives quite so readily. With the battle clearly lost, they started to break away and made their escape, with the Normans snapping at their heels. As the sun set, some were lucky enough to reach the cover of the forest, others were trampled under war-horse hooves, slashed by swords, or skewered by lances.

Just at this moment, English reinforcements may have started to arrive; too late to save Harold, but certainly not too late to give the Normans a nasty surprise. Whether they were fresh troops or just men determined to make a last stand, the English seem to have occupied a strong position on Caldbeck Hill.

They stood on the edge of a steep gully and among ditches on the edge of a wood. The gully was deep and covered with low undergrowth and brambles. It may even have been part of the earthworks of an ancient fort. It would become known as *Malfosse* – Evil Ditch – by the Normans.

It was getting dark and the Normans were giddy with the bloodlust of hunting down the fleeing Englishmen. They charged towards the woods, but before they knew what was happening, the Norman knights were riding their war-horses straight over the edge of the unseen gully and careering down to the bottom. Horses stumbled and fell, the horses behind falling over the ones in front, trampling on the bodies of thrown knights, breaking legs and necks, and tumbling into a chaos of flailing limbs. The English were on hand to finish them off.

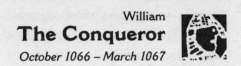

THE NORMAN KNIGHTS spurred on their horses – and on they came, in total chaos, one after another until there was no room for any more to get to the bottom of the ditch and the riders at the back finally woke up to what was happening in front of them. William arrived to find Eustace of Boulogne about to beat a hasty retreat with 50 of his knights.

The story goes that as William was forcefully ordering him to turn about and get at the English, Eustace was wounded; hit between the shoulder blades, and blood started pouring out from his nose and mouth. So William wheeled round his horse and led the attack himself, once again stamping his authority on his men and crushing resistance in the enemy.

It was dark now, and pursuit of the English into the forest would have been madness. William rode back to the battlefield and pitched camp for the night. All around his tent were the bloody bodies of those who had fallen in the day's fighting. The coming night at least provided a little relief from the grim view. But this was a traditional thing to do; to take possession of the battlefield. William took off his armour and received the cheers of his men. They had won. England was theirs!

At sunrise they began burying their Norman dead. Saxon women came forward in a sad and sobbing procession, asking for the bodies of their loved ones; of their husbands, sons, brothers; asking for the chance to bury them properly. William granted their requests. He could afford to be generous, after all. And it was a matter of honour. Having said that, the bulk of the English dead were left as food for scavengers; the ravens, the rats, the wolves and the foxes. Once picked clean, the bones would lie heaped up as a chilling victory display.

Now William ordered that Harold's body, or what was left of it, should be fetched. Not surprisingly, the Normans given the task had trouble trying to decide which of the fallen English was Harold. Although some of the Normans would have been able to recognize Harold alive – he had been to Normandy only a couple of years before – he had probably been pretty hacked about by the knights who took the hill. If we believe the version that has him attacked by a hit squad of knights, then he had been disembowelled, dismembered, beheaded and possibly castrated.

But Edith Swan-neck was at the battlefield. She had the unenviable task of identifying the corpse of the man she loved. It must have been a shattering experience for her. We have no way of knowing how many corpses Edith looked at before she found the body of her fallen king, so mutilated it was unrecognizable to all but her. Perhaps Harold's body was found with an arrow in the eye and the legend began there.

A request arrived from Harold's mother, Gytha, saying that if William would give up her son's body she would give him Harold's weight in gold. Gytha had lost her husband and five of her sons – four of them in the same month – and another, Wulfnoth, was still held prisoner in Normandy. Now she had lost her country. She must have been devastated, but William refused.

It was said that Harold's mauled body was given to a half-English knight, William Malet, to be buried. It was also said that it was wrapped in royal purple and carried down to the beach to be buried under a cairn (a pile of stones) at the base of a cliff, the Normans joking that he could rest there to guard the shores he had tried so hard to defend. It sounds childish and spiteful; childish and spiteful enough to be true.

William stayed at Hastings for the next few days, burying his dead, tending to the wounded, resting his men and sending for reinforcements. Harold was dead. His brothers Gyrth, Leofwine and Tostig were dead. Harald Hardrada was dead. The only remaining problem for William was Edgar the Aetheling, the remaining heir to the Wessex line of English kings.

And sure enough, those traitorous brothers, Morcar and Edwin, had arrived in London (having seemingly changed their minds about William) and together with Archbishop Ealdred, encouraged the *witangemot* to vote in young Edgar as the new king in defiance of the invading William. But the coronation was delayed until Christmas, leaving England without a king, and William firmly ashore.

William was not pleased when no word came from London. With Harold gone and his brothers with him, William might have expected England to collapse and give him the crown. Still, if that was how they wanted to play it, so be it. On 20 October, the Norman army had regrouped and were on the move again.

The first stop was Romney, in Kent, where the inhabitants were about to pay the price for killing a handful of Normans who landed there by mistake during William's invasion. England got its first taste of William's tried and tested terror tactics, with brutal torture and executions. This was the Norman army in action. This is what lay in store for England.

Dover was next in line and despite having good defences, the town gave in without a struggle once it heard what had gone on at Romney. But that did not save Dover from the rampaging soldiers. William's over-enthusiastic troops set fire to the place – perhaps Eustace of Boulogne was taking revenge for the attack on his men in 1051. Surprisingly, William offered to pay for rebuilding work.

The Normans did not quite have it all their way – many of the men were now struck down by illness; possibly dysentery. But William's army was able to march on without a problem and without any losses – there were no castles in England to slow him down and make him stop for lengthy sieges; something William would soon put right. He now made for Canterbury – the religious capital of England. The town gave in without a struggle, its people swearing allegiance to William.

At Canterbury, though, William's progress *was* halted when he fell ill. The Normans were forced to stay a month, as William was very sick and close to death. But, as so often on this venture, he escaped death's clutches again.

At the end of November William was well enough to lead the march on London. The old Roman road of Watling Street would have taken William straight there from Canterbury, but instead he took a longer route, circling round the city like a lion round a wounded prey.

He moved west and sent a force of his knights to test the English defences. Was there any fight left in the English? Well, yes there was. Finally the Normans did meet some resistance. William's knights clashed with English troops sent across the Thames by the city of London.

The Normans torched Southwark in retaliation before rejoining the rest of the advance moving west. William stayed to the south of the Thames, smashing his way through Surrey, Hampshire and Berkshire, leaving a trail of destruction behind him.

William then sent a force to Winchester, the ancient capital of the old kingdom of Wessex, held by Queen Edith, Edward's widow and Harold's sister. Queen Edith had taken Tostig's side in the Godwinson brothers' argument and must have been devastated at the news that Tostig had been killed by Harold's men at Stamford Bridge.

Perhaps, out of spite, she welcomed William as Harold's killer; or perhaps after losing her husband and four brothers in the space of a year, she had ceased to care. Whatever the reason, she offered her submission to William.

William moved on towards the River Thames. Most of the infantry used the crossing at Goring for the Ridgeway track, while he and the knights crossed on the Icknield Way at Wallingford, about 50 miles west of London.

Stigand, the Archbishop of Canterbury, turned up to meet him and put himself at William's mercy, swearing allegiance to him, and dropping his earlier support for Edgar. Perhaps he believed that God had chosen William to be king and punished Harold for his sins. Or perhaps he just wanted to keep his job. Again, whatever the true reason, just as with Edith, this was a huge blow to English morale.

William had his men build a wooden castle inside the walls of Wallingford and continued on his way, travelling north-east along the ancient Icknield Way, sending scouting parties ahead to watch for signs of an English ambush.

Eventually, in December, he was near Hertford, about 20 miles north of London. William and his men had hammered, hacked and burned their way along in a huge arc, terrifying everyone in their path. Although William's force was relatively small, the nerve of London finally snapped.

When William reached the village of Little Berkhamsted, east of Hertford, he was met by a reception committee; not of armed men but of broken men. The teenage Edgar the Aetheling, so recently voted king, had decided that it might, after all, be better if he gave up that honour.

With him were Ealdred, Archbishop of York, and other English leaders resigned to make their submission to the Duke. Those self-serving northern earls, Morcar and Edwin, were also there, still hoping, no doubt, that William would leave them in their earldoms.

This may seem a little cowardly, but really most of these men probably felt as if they had very little choice. Some may have even hoped to spare the country more destruction. Not all men are made to fight. They seemed to have felt that God was punishing them, just as King Edward had prophesied.

Really, a lot of the blame for this collapse of English resistance must rest with Harold. Not only had he made the mistake of going to Hastings without enough men, but he had taken Gyrth and Leofwine with him. Harold should either have put the army under the command of his brothers and stayed in London, or led the army and left his brothers in London. Now the men who could have organized an effective counterattack or even have been considered as possible kings in their own right were dead.

The English leaders swore oaths of allegiance to William and gave him hostages, and William smiled and promised he would be a "*kind lord*" to them. This seemed very, *very* unlikely.

William must have enjoyed seeing the English crumble but, strangely, rather than snatch the crown for himself straight away, he called a council meeting and took some advice. He was wary of becoming king too soon, when he still had not conquered the whole country. But his advisers – and the English leaders – told him to make himself king right away. The country needed some leadership if it wasn't going to collapse into civil war with the north of England seizing its opportunity to break away from the conquered south.

But William was as cautious as ever. He sent an advance party into the capital to build a fort; a fort that would one day become the Tower of London. When he was sure it was safe, William entered the city of London.

William made arrangements for his coronation and on Christmas Day 1066 he was crowned king in Edward's abbey church in Westminster. William refused to have

Archbishop Stigand preside over the ceremony, and so it was left to Ealdred – the Archbishop of York who had crowned Harold – to do it.

Ealdred insisted that William swear an oath on the Bible that he would:

> . . . rule all this people as well as the best of kings before him,
> if they were to be loyal to him.

William agreed, swore, and Ealdred placed the crown on William's head. It had been a long journey: from William the Bastard to William the Conqueror, and finally, William, King of England.

Ealdred then asked the Englishmen gathered there if they accepted William as their king. They did and without hesitation; though probably not "*joyfully*" as the Normans would have us believe. Then the Bishop of Coutances asked the Normans the same thing, and not surprisingly they also accepted William as King of England.

But William's troops were the eleventh-century equivalent of trigger-happy, and when they heard the shouts of acclaim coming from the church, they managed, without much evidence, to convince themselves that the English were rioting. There may even have been some resistance that the Normans later covered up. Perhaps someone shouted "Go home, Normans!" or just called out Harold's name. Whatever the cause, they used it as an excuse to have a riot of their own, slashing at any passing Saxons, burning the local houses and looting property. People ran out of the church to see what was going on, as firelight flickered outside the church windows and screams filled the air.

As he sat there on the throne he had fought so hard to win, William was visibly shaking. Along with his reaction to the news of Harold's coronation almost a year before, it was one of the few times that William showed any emotion. But whether he was trembling with joy, relief or fear, we will never know.

William had Harold's Fighting Man standard sent to the Pope in Rome. The England of Harold Godwinson seemed to have been crushed and, once more, a foreigner had been crowned king of the English.

Well, sort of. Really, William was only king of *south-east* England – at least that was the only area of England he held by force of arms. While Normandy celebrated William's victory, William himself knew that it was a long way from being over.

William tried to live up to the oath he had made at his coronation. He tried to discipline his men and forbade them to drink in taverns in an effort to stop them going on drunken rampages, and he ordered them stay within the law. No more killing Englishmen just for the fun of it.

William made his half-brother, Bishop Odo, Earl of Kent with William fitzOsbern as his deputy. He wanted someone he could trust there, guarding the port of Dover. William needed Odo, because he was returning to Normandy. He might be King of England now, but that did not mean he could just forget about Normandy, with its history of rebellions. William was to end up sailing back and forth across the Channel in the years to come, ever mindful of the need to keep both countries in check personally.

William left for Normandy in March 1067 and did not return to England until the following winter. He must have been a little concerned that his grip over the English had been kept in place while he was away, after all, the conquest had barely begun. England was not going to be taken without *any* resistance.

Strangely, though, the first serious rebellion William had to deal with in England was not from the English at all. While William's deputies in England were dealing with some local aggravation north of the Thames, William's ally, Eustace of Boulogne – the same Eustace, brother-in-law of Edward the Confessor, who had caused the trouble in Dover – decided to make a traitorous play for power.

Eustace came by sea to Dover aided by the men of Kent, who were happy to seize any chance to attack the Normans. But the Normans were more than a match for them. William's men in Dover beat off the attack, Eustace's nephew was captured, and Eustace was forced to escape by ship while the Dover garrison pursued and killed many of the attackers. England was not quite conquered yet.

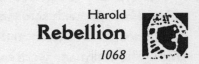

IT WAS CLEAR that not all Englishmen were prepared to let themselves be ruled by the Normans. William's men were ambushed. Rebellions broke out. It was Harold's memory and his remaining family that inspired many of the rebels and Exeter began to be a focus for some of those fighting back.

Harold's mother, Gytha, lived in Exeter and while her daughter, Queen Edith, was a figurehead for the English collapse at Winchester, Gytha stood as a symbol of the English resistance. When William returned to England, he went to deal with her.

Early in 1068 William and his men stood outside the city walls of Exeter demanding the town's surrender. He had taken hostages and to show them that he was not going to take no for an answer, he had one of the hostages blinded in full view of the townsfolk – perhaps it was a symbolic reference to Harold's blinding at Hastings.

This typically brutal act may have had the opposite effect, however, as it seemed to strengthen the resolve of the people of Exeter, and they refused to open the gates. The Normans were experts at sieges – they had had lots of practice. Eventually Gytha Godwinson and Exeter surrendered. William had a castle built in this unruly town immediately.

With his mother defeated, Harold Godwinson's fight was continued by his teenage sons, Godwin, Edmund and Magnus, who attacked the south-west from Ireland. They attacked Somerset in 1068 and in 1069 attacked Exeter, but they were boys. They were never going to be a serious threat to William.

Eventually they were sent packing back to Ireland. Their grandmother, Gytha, left Exeter to die in bitter exile. The Godwinsons were finished. Harold would not be avenged.

Death of the Conqueror
1069 – 1087

DESPITE THE FACT that he had led Morcar to believe he might keep his earldom, William had put Tostig's old deputy, Copsig, in charge of Northumbria. The last thing the Northumbrians wanted was to be reminded of the hated Tostig. Like so many before him, William was about to find what a hornet's nest the north of England really was. The Northumbrians murdered Copsig just as soon as William left the country.

But the northerners were dealing with William the Conqueror now. When he returned he went north in person. Despite submitting to William, the slippery Edwin and Morcar were causing trouble and had allied themselves to their Welsh nephew, Bleddyn. As William's men were building a castle at Warwick, though, the earls turned up and submitted to William again.

William built a castle at Nottingham, and York surrendered. William built a castle at York, and Malcolm III of Scotland decided it would be diplomatic to make peace with William through the Bishop of Durham. William now turned south, building castles at Lincoln, Huntingdon and Cambridge on route.

But it was never going to be that simple, even for William. In 1069, everyone with a grudge took a shot at the Normans, launching themselves from the unconquered north. Edgar the Aetheling was there with his brother-in-law, Malcolm III of Scotland, with whom he had taken shelter. The Northumbrians rose up in arms and Swein Estrithson, the King of Denmark, sent ships and men to support Earl Waltheof, Siward of Northumbria's son, who had been a child when Tostig Godwinson snatched his father's earldom.

On 28 January 1069 the northern rebels launched an attack against William's new Earl of Northumbria, Robert of Commines. The rebels hit the Normans early in the morning at Durham and Robert was killed.

A Norman force under Robert fitzRichard decided to go for glory and launch an attack on the rebels from the Northumbrian capital of York, but the Normans were routed and massacred. William was out of the country again, in Normandy, but returned to answer a plea for help from William Malet and the Norman survivors trapped in York by the advancing Northumbrians.

William went straight to York with a force of men, just as Harold had done in 1066. The rebels made a run for it and William retook the city. He decided that one castle was not enough for such a troublesome place and had another built.

No sooner had William returned south, though, than a huge Danish fleet appeared and started attacking and plundering the north-east coast. Just as Harald Hardrada had done, the Danes sailed into the Humber, and just as the Norse had done, they headed for York, meeting up with Edgar the Aetheling on route.

William went north again, taking a detour to sort out a revolt in Staffordshire. The Danes refused to meet him in open battle and William paid them to leave. He could afford to, so why waste the energy and men in fighting? William celebrated Christmas in York. Then he set about making the north pay for its impudence.

Harrying had been seen before, but not with the ruthless and heartless efficiency that the Normans put into it. To harry meant to destroy everything, to make the land uninhabitable, and William was an expert. Houses and crops were destroyed, and livestock was slaughtered in a huge swathe.

William's men fanned out and searched every inch of land, driving out the rebels and leaving them no hiding place or food to eat, burning everything in their path until the land north of the Humber was a desert of ash, and thousands of villagers were left homeless.

The severity of William's attack was shocking, even by the standards of the day. England had never seen anything like this before. It was said that people were reduced to eating dogs, cats, rats, and even human flesh to survive.

Englishmen rebelled against their Norman conquerors up and down the land, but in every case, William and his generals simply outwitted and outmatched the opposition. England was conquered. Except, that is, for one last pocket of resistance...

Harold Godwinson's Wessex had fallen and now the fiercely independent Northumbria had been conquered, too. It was left to another of the old kingdoms to make a stand – East Anglia, the area that had once been under the protection of Harold's brother, Gyrth. It was here that a legend was born; the legend of Hereward the Wake.

Hereward was probably a *thegn* and possibly a king's *thegn*. He held manors in Lincolnshire and may have been outlawed for attacking a Norman lord, but very little can be known for sure.

The rebellion in East Anglia also features those earls who have dogged this whole story – Morcar and Edwin. William is said to have offered Edwin his daughter's hand in marriage, but changed his mind (possibly after finding out what treacherous characters Edwin and his brother were). Edwin took this as a real insult and was close to rebelling with Welsh allies.

In 1071, realizing too late what a ruthless man William was, Earl Morcar joined Hereward and the revolt in East Anglia. The rebels were holed up on the misty Isle of Ely.

The fens had yet to be drained, and Ely really was an island in those days, surrounded by creeks and marshes.

William attacked the rebels with his usual relentlessness, building a causeway through the marshes. The rebels fled if they could, and Hereward managed to escape and disappeared into legend where he became a kind of Robin Hood-like symbol of English resistance.

Morcar surrendered and submitted to William – *again* – but William was not about to give Morcar another chance. He was thrown into a dungeon where he spent the rest of his days. Edwin tried to get a force together to get his brother out, but was betrayed and killed before he could do it.

So ended the lives of two men whose scheming and selfishness had done as much as anyone else to bring about the conquest of England. It was they who had stirred up trouble against Tostig in Northumbria and thereby caused the feud between him and Harold. Because of that feud Tostig sought the help of Harald Hardrada. And because Hardrada invaded, Harold had been forced to defend England on two fronts at once, hurtling back and forth from London to Yorkshire and meeting William, ill-prepared and with depleted forces; forces that were made smaller still by Morcar and Edwin's non-appearance at Hastings. The brothers could not have done more to ensure the success of William's invasion if they had been Norman themselves.

Originally William had allowed those English nobles who submitted to his authority before he took the crown to hold their positions, but before long he had replaced the entire English ruling class with men of his own choosing from the other side of the Channel.

Hordes of Norman and French nobles came over as colonists, bringing their families and servants with them, seeing a chance to make something of themselves in a new country. But there was huge resentment among the colonized English.

William and the Normans destroyed whole swathes of England, harrying in pursuit of rebels as they had done in the north. It caused misery and famine as they systematically wrecked and redeveloped settlements to build their castles. Taxes were raised with ruthless efficiency to pay for this and, not surprisingly, collectors were hated.

The Normans were way ahead of the English in building fortifications. At first these castles were wooden, but eventually they were built from stone. And just as William went in for castle-building on a huge scale, he also built churches up and down the country, often replacing and erasing earlier English churches. The Normans built abbeys – including Battle Abbey to commemorate the victory at Hastings – and they built huge and imposing cathedrals that dominated the skyline for miles around.

Just as English earls were replaced by Norman and French barons, so English bishops, too, were gradually replaced. Archbishop Stigand had submitted to William as he headed to London after the invasion and was rewarded by being allowed to keep hold of his job in Canterbury, but only until 1070, when he was replaced by Lanfranc, the man who had helped William get the Pope's support before the invasion.

William changed the nature of the English army, too. The elite force would no longer be *thegns* or axe-wielding *huscarls*, they would be knights, and cavalrymen would be the elite of the army for centuries to come.

To see just what he had conquered, William commissioned the *Domesday Book* in 1086, a kind of census; a record of everything in the country, who lived there, what they owned and so on. It also showed the devastation his men had caused as village after village appears with the word *wasta*, meaning "wasted", next to it.

William certainly never seems to have had the chance to enjoy his reign as King of England. He continued to have problems back in Normandy, both with his son who wanted to rule Normandy himself, and from the rulers of France and Anjou, who were worried about William's growing power. In July 1087 he launched one of his signature surprise attacks against rebels at Mantes. William won the battle, but was injured as he and his men sacked the town. The injury proved fatal and, on 9 September 1087, William died.

William had become very overweight in his later life and when they tried to get his body into his stone tomb at Caen, it burst. A foul stench leaked out into the church and into the nostrils of those who had come to pay their respects. So ended the life of William the Conqueror.

The Last Word

IT SEEMED AS IF the England of Wessex and the Godwins was gone for ever. This was Year Zero of a new regime. When the next King Edward took the throne in 1272 he became known as Edward I – Edward, son of Alfred the Great, or even Edward the Confessor didn't count because they were *English* – they were pre-conquest; pre-Norman; pre-William the Conqueror.

But perhaps King Harold II can have the final word here, because his story did not quite end at the Battle of Hastings. The Normans say that William had him buried on the shore at Hastings, but did he?

Once again, it is not what is true that is always the most important thing, but what people believe and why. The English needed something to believe in. William had conquered the country, but not their hearts or their imaginations. In their dreams and stories and poems they could still be free.

By the twelfth century it was said that William had been shamed into accepting Harold's mother's request for her son's body, and it had in fact been taken to the abbey he founded at Waltham and buried there.

The story was that Harold had taken two churchmen with him from Waltham to the battle and these two churchmen had asked William for the body. This may have been Waltham Abbey's way of attracting extra pilgrims – pilgrims were always in the market for buying souvenirs – but a cult certainly did grow up around the memory of Harold, with its focus at Waltham Abbey.

There were those who said that Harold should be patron saint of England – a position filled by the pious Edward the Confessor, who was patron saint for many years before being replaced by St George.

The English even told a story that Harold had been thrown mistakenly among the dead and was found, still breathing, by a group of women who looked after him at a nearby cottage and that he lived to a ripe old age. Maybe Edith Swan-neck had identified another body on purpose to throw the Normans off the scent. After all, it was said that no one could recognize the mutilated body but her. From there, the story continues, he went on to Winchester, where he supposedly hid in a cellar for two years before getting back to full strength and leaving the country.

One story has it that Harold not only survived, but waged a war of resistance against the Norman oppressors until he gave up the sword for the cross and a life of religious devotion. Some stories even claimed he came back to England to live as a hermit in the cliffs near Dover, before wandering off into Shropshire and living unrecognized under the assumed name of "Christian". He covered his face with a cloth to conceal his identity and was led about like a blind man. Or maybe he *was* blind; blind from that arrow wound at Hastings. This is all incredibly unlikely, of course, but like so much of this story, impossible to prove or disprove.

One of these stories ends with Harold spending the rest of his life in a chapel outside the city walls of Chester, finally confessing on his deathbed that he was in fact Harold Godwinson, the last Saxon king of England.

Afterword

SO WAS HAROLD the rightful King of England? The simple answer is yes. Edward the Confessor put the country in his charge and the *witangemot* voted Harold in. Even if William really did believe he deserved to be king, England did not want *him*.

The eleventh century was a superstitious age, however, and many people, English and Norman, will have assumed that Harold's defeat was a judgement by God. Kings held power *"by the grace of God"* and God seemed to have chosen William.

But whatever happened to Harold, it was certainly not the death of Anglo-Saxon England. The Normans did a good job of trying to erase all signs of the culture of the people whose land they now ruled, but they did not succeed. The familiar English pattern of village, manor house, market town and church was not a Norman invention. It was already there before the invasion. More than half of the parish churches that existed in the year 1700 had been founded *before* 1066.

The *Domesday Book* that William commissioned was an impressive achievement, but it was the English system of government that enabled him to do it. The English system of separately governed shires was so effective that it still exists today. And perhaps the biggest memorial to the English world of Harold Godwinson lies in its language, for despite the Norman invasion, despite the Battle of Hastings, despite William the Conqueror, the English speak English, not French.

A few years after William's death the events of 1066 were immortalized in a work of art – the famous Bayeux Tapestry; not actually a tapestry at all, but a fantastic piece of embroidery, telling the story in 70 scenes, from Harold's supposed visit and oath in Normandy in 1064, to the furious Battle of Hastings.

It may even have been commissioned by William's half-brother Odo, the Bishop of Bayeux – who was actually there at the battle. Ironically although the Bayeux Tapestry may have been commissioned by a *Norman*, and tells the story of the Battle of Hastings from a Norman point of view, it was probably actually made in England.

The beauty of the design and the stylization of the figures means that at first the awfulness of its content is not apparent. Look closer and you will see severed heads and dismembered corpses in the border. Beautiful though it is, the Bayeux Tapestry is also a shocking reminder of the horrors of war; and of that fateful autumn day in 1066.

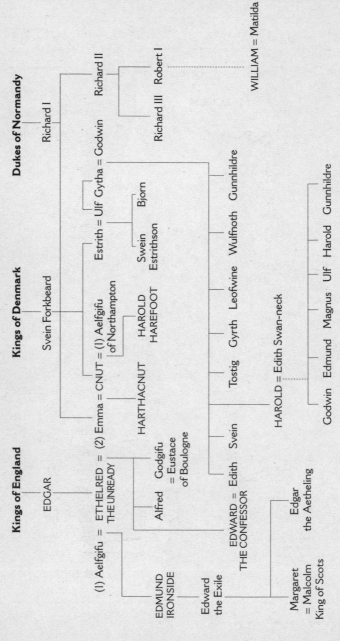

134

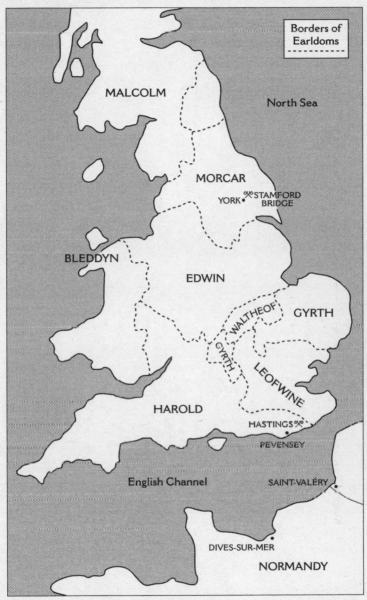

England in 1066

Further Reading

For a contemporary view of the world of Harold and William try: *The Anglo-Saxon Chronicles* edited by Michael Swanton (Phoenix Press, 2000) which were written by monks living at the time.

For a short but detailed modern view of Anglo-Saxon history, try: *The Anglo-Saxon Age: A Very Short Introduction* by John Blair (Oxford 1984).

The Anglo-Saxons by James Campbell (Penguin 1991) is a large format book with lots of pictures.

For a short and illustrated look at the Normans and their world try: *The Normans* by David Nicolle and Angus McBride (Osprey 1987).

Hastings 1066: The Fall of Saxon England by Christopher Gravett (Osprey 1992) is very good on the details of the battle and has lots of maps and illustrations of weapons and armour.

1066: The Year of Three Battles by Frank McLynn (Pimlico 1999) is very detailed and is particularly good for anyone who wants to know more about the extraordinary Harald Hardrada.

In Search of the Dark Ages by Michael Woods (BBC Books 1981) has a very good chapter on the events surrounding the Battle of Hastings and has chapters on Alfred the Great and Ethelred the Unready.

1066 The Year of the Conquest by David Howarth (reprinted as Classic Penguin 2002) is a wonderfully written and very readable look at the people and events of 1066.

For a fascinating insight into the everyday lives of the people living in eleventh century England try: *1000: What Life was Like at the Turn of the First Millennium* by Robert Lacey and Danny Danziger (Abacus 2000).

Or why not get into the Anglo-Saxon mind by reading the heroic poem *Beowulf* or better still, listen to Seamus Heaney reading his own translation of the poem: *Beowulf* translated by Seamus Heaney (Faber and Faber 1999) or as an audiotape (Penguin Audiobooks 2000).

Acknowledgements

Picture insert

1 Harold crowned King of England: detail from the Bayeux Tapestry – 11th Century by special permission of the City of Bayeux

2 Halley's Comet over Harold's court: detail from the Bayeux Tapestry – 11th Century by special permission of the City of Bayeux

3 William's men loading ships: detail from the Bayeux Tapestry – 11th Century by special permission of the City of Bayeux

4 William's army crossing the Channel: detail from the Bayeux Tapestry – 11th Century by special permission of the City of Bayeux

5 William's men building castle at Hastings: detail from the Bayeux Tapestry – 11th Century by special permission of the City of Bayeux

Family tree of the Kings of England and Denmark, and the Dukes of Normandy by Michelle Hearne

Map of England in 1066 by Michelle Hearne

Index

Emma, Queen (wife of Cnut and Ethelred) 12, 21, 27

Enguerrand of Ponthieu 30, 99

Ethelred the Unready, King 9, 12, 20-1, 27, 50

Eustace of Boulogne 13, 15-16, 88, 93, 106, 109, 116

fitzOsbern, William 25, 28, 88, 115

fitzWymark, Robert 7, 10, 86

fyrd/fyrdsmen 44, 46, 50, 58-9, 66, 77, 84, 90, 96, 98, 104

Godwin, Earl of Wessex (father of Harold) 12-14, 16-19, 24, 33, 88

Guy of Ponthieu 32

Gyrth Godwinson (brother of Harold) 47, 50, 82-4, 90, 92, 97, 108, 112, 122

Gytha (mother of Harold) 108, 117, 118

Hakon (nephew of Harold) 17, 33, 35, 84

Harald Hardrada, King of Norway 60-9, 77, 84-5, 87, 103, 108, 121, 123

Harold Harefoot, King 12-13

Harthacnut, King 12-13, 27

Hastings 76-9, 82-4, 87, 91, 97, 99, 108, 112, 118, 123, 127, 129, 131

hauberks *see* chainmail

Henry I, King of France 28-32, 99

Hereward the Wake 122

horses 49-50, 54-7, 72, 74, 78, 88, 95-7, 99, 105-6

huscarls 48-9, 52, 55, 59, 61, 63, 65, 80-1, 84, 86, 90-1, 95, 101, 104, 125

infantry 54, 95

knights 55-6, 78-9, 93, 97, 101, 103, 105-7, 125

Lanfranc 36-7, 125

Leofric, Earl of Mercia 18, 23

Leofwine Godwinson (brother of Harold) 17, 43, 47, 49, 84, 90, 94, 97, 108, 112

Malcolm III, King of Scotland 43, 120

Malet, William 108, 120

Margot, Hugh 82, 87

Matilda (wife of William) 30, 34, 51

mercenaries 49, 56, 62, 68, 84